# Women of Steel
a Living History of Corby

Written and Directed by Paula Boulton

CORBYZONE

Originally published in Great Britain in 2008 by Corby Zone in edition of 1500 copies
Typeset in Optima 10 and 11 pt size.

Printed in Corby by Impress Print
Unit 6, The Grove, Corby, Northamptonshire NN18 8EW
www.impress-print.co.uk

A CIP catalogue record for this title is available from the British Library

ISBN 13: 9781906482008

10th Anniversary Edition reprinted by CompletelyNovel.com in 2018

Book Layout and Design by Kenneth James Martin
www.kennethmartin.co.uk

Copyright © 2008 by Paula Boulton
positivepaula2@aol.com

The right of Paula Boulton to be identified as the Author of the Work has been asserted by her in accordance with the Copyright, Designs and Patents Act 1988.

All rights reserved. No part of this publication may be reproduced, stored in a retrieval system, or transmitted, in any form or by any means, electronic, mechanical, photocopying, recording or otherwise, without the prior permission of the publisher.

Any resemblance to any persons either living or dead is entirely deliberate.
Without prejudice - E & O E

## CONTENTS

Preface by Ann-Marie Lawson . . . . . . . . v
Introduction by Paula Boulton . . . . . . . vii
Cast in order of appearance . . . . . . . xiv

Act One: The Rise and Fall of Steel 1930 - 1979 . . . . 1
Prelude to Act One, Song: Village Life . . . . . 3
Scene 1: In the Beginning . . . . . . . . 7
Song: Jobs May Come . . . . . . . . . 8
Scene 2: Roots . . . . . . . . . . 9
Scene 3: Homesick, 1934 . . . . . . . . 23
Song: Accidents . . . . . . . . . . 27
Scene 4: The Widow, 1960 . . . . . . . . 29
Scene 5: One Woman of Steel . . . . . . . 33
Scene 6: Cleaners in the Quantivac, 1960 . . . . . 43
Scene 7: A Canteen Worker, Plugmill Canteen, 1974 . . . 53
Song: As The Works Grows, So the Town Grows . . . 57
Scene 8: Corby New Town in its Heyday . . . . . 65
Scene 9: Union Meeting, Canteen, 1979 . . . . . 73
Scene 10: ROSAC Demonstration, London, 28th June 1979 . . 89
Song: Keep the Candle Burning . . . . . . . 89
Scene 11: The End of Steel . . . . . . . . 93

Act Two: WonderWorld, WonderWhen? 1984 . . . . 101
Prelude to Act Two, Song: WonderWorld . . . . . 103
Scene 1: Enterprise Zone . . . . . . . . 105
Scene 2: Broken Dreams . . . . . . . . 109
Song: Broken Dreams . . . . . . . . . 111
Scene 3: The Aftermath . . . . . . . . 113
Scene 4: Stand Your Ground . . . . . . . 129
Song: Sweatshop . . . . . . . . . . 130
Song: WonderWorld (Reprise) . . . . . . . 138
Wasted Years, 1990 - 2005 . . . . . . . . 139
Scene 5: A chocolate factory in Corby 1998 *by Emma Boulton Roe* . 139

| | |
|---|---|
| The Present Day | 153 |
| Scene 6: Steel Kids | 153 |
| Scene 7: The Future | 159 |
| Scene 8: I Wish *by Kirsty Graham* | 167 |
| Scene 9: 'Til the End *by Jack Boulton Roe* | 170 |
| Scene 10: A Cut Above | 175 |
| Scene 11: Hope for the Future | 181 |
| Song: Give Us a Job to Do in Corby | 183 |
| | |
| Author's Notes | 185 |
| Contents of Author's Notes | 186 |
| | |
| Miscellaneous | 248 |
| Creative Process and Afterword | 248 |
| Cast Lists | 256 |
| Comments from Cast Members | 259 |
| East Carlton Park Programme | 261 |
| Additional Song Lyrics | 269 |
| Audience Feedback from East Carlton Park | 279 |
| Arc Theatre Programme | 283 |
| MP's Letter of Endorsement | 289 |
| | |
| Funders | 290 |
| Acknowledgements | 292 |
| Photo Credits | 293 |
| Bibliography / Further Reading | 294 |

# PREFACE
## by Ann-Marie Lawson

As winner of the *Spirit of Corby* award 2008, I was invited to write this Preface. I am honoured to oblige, as I am the daughter of a Steelworker, and was also a Steelworks Employee for twenty-eight years, witnessing first-hand the era that the book records.

*Women of Steel* is a story of reality and truth that shows the integral part that these women played in the identity of Corby town. Corby became synonymous with Steelmaking, and in doing so created a culture of achievement and comfort for the Working Classes.

The book captures the ethos and values of the era - from recognising the melting-pot of cultural diversity in Corby, to acknowledging the price that Workers paid for a decent standard of living. Men did not realise the effect the Working Conditions and Shift patterns were having on their health. Even if they had known, many would still say it was worth it. The camaraderie was tangible and, as many men found out after the Closure of The Steelworks, it was irreplaceable and impossible to manufacture.

The book shows the selflessness of the women as they supported their men, paying little regard to their own homesickness or the depression they often felt. While the men were working to provide a decent standard of living for their families, the *Women of Steel* became the backbone on which this town was built. These women had a contentment that is hard to find nowadays, because community life was strong and the commonalities between the women were evident.

There were, of course, women who Worked in the Industry, but they often held Jobs deemed to be of less importance than those of the men. The Works was a self-contained principality - a patriarchal society that needed women to hold the threads together, whilst keeping them in stereotypical female roles, thus maintaining the status quo and allowing the men to embrace positions of power.

In 1980, with the threat of Closure of The Steelworks, the town came together in a way that made me proud and showed me what solidarity meant and how it felt. This feeling has stayed with me, and although I have had to defend Corby many times in different arenas, I can do so with confidence, remembering that raw emotion with very little effort. We genuinely believed that if there were no struggle there would be no progress, and we were prepared to fight to save our Steelworks. I never saw any apathy throughout those times, just a genuine will to succeed, and even in the end there was an acceptance of what we had fought to change but ultimately could not. We were united in our belief that the blame lay firmly with the conservative government, but more significantly with Margaret

Thatcher – she may have been the "Iron Lady" but she was not a Woman of Steel! When The Works closed in 1980, the demographic of the town changed for ever. Change had come too quickly, and psychologically, socially and financially many were not prepared for the change that had rocked their world.

Corby women, however, are fighters, and for many women the Closure of The Steelworks provided opportunities for them to develop as women and embrace their individuality. There appeared to be more opportunities for women to enter the Workplace and use the skills that came naturally to them through managing households to improve their own career opportunities. The future for young people had in the past meant either life as a Steelworker living in Corby, or an academic education that enabled you to move onwards and upwards, leaving Corby behind. In my experience this is changing: young people now can achieve academic success and bring it back to the town, where it can be rewarded with sound career prospects and advancement. Corby is on the up, and I am proud to have lived here through all the changes and survived. We will always be *Women of Steel* because we are a fundamental part of the structure on which Corby was built, changed and reborn. We are the link between the past, the present and the future, and have a duty to inspire our children to thrive and prosper in a town they not only call home, but one they are proud to belong to.

This book portrays real-life experiences and insights, showing women Working together behind the scenes, supporting each other to realise their aspirations, hopes and dreams. In continuing to do so they are contributing to a modern multicultural society in which hopefully everyone can learn, live, Work and socialise with others, free from exclusion, prejudice, discrimination, harassment and violence.

Paula Boulton is a true woman of Corby: a woman whose integrity shines through adversity, a woman who tells it like it is, and in doing so, humbles us all. This book is a testament to Paula, who understands that if there is no struggle there is no progress, that if we want freedom we need to understand oppression and its many different forms, and that if we want to swim in the ocean we have to accept the awful roar of its many waters. It is to be hoped that the upcoming generation of *Women of Steel* find Paula an inspiring rôle model.

Ann-Marie Lawson
June 2008

# INTRODUCTION

The Steelworks in Corby closed in April 1980. This single event changed history, our history - the living history of the people of this town.

Twenty-five years later, I decided that, as an Arts Worker, not a Steelworker, I wanted to forge something from this history as a lasting memorial. And so *Women of Steel* was born. A living, breathing set of stories which capture something of the heart of the town.

It has gone through various transformations since its inception.

First it was a multi-media site-specific play, performed at Corby's Steel Heritage Centre, East Carlton Park, in July 2006. The various scenes were performed, sometimes simultaneously, in different parts of the building and outdoors. The audience moved around from one to the other.

Corby Women's Theatre Group (CWTHG) and Shout! Youth Theatre worked together with the Orebits band to perform the piece, with guest appearances from some of the Steelmen who had marched to London with the Save Our Steel Petition in 1979.

The event was a resounding success and led to *Stories of Steel*, a project designed to reach a wider audience and preserve the stories and images for posterity.

The first part of this process was the rewriting of the play in a more traditional style for indoor performance. It was performed at the Arc Theatre in March 2007 for two nights, to sell-out audiences.

This version was subsequently filmed in June 2007 and was released as a DVD in June 2008. An exhibition of photos used in the production, and of the performances, was staged in December 2007 at the Willows Arts Centre.

And now the final version of *Women of Steel* is this, the book.

I use the term "book" loosely. As a synthesis of a playscript and a photograph album, it feels like an unusual and innovative format. Some readers will look first at the pictures, others will focus on the text. However you approach it, this book is the manifestation of our heartfelt desire to encapsulate the myriad of true stories and images amassed throughout the *Women of Steel* process. We present them to you, the reader, in a portable package you can keep forever!

A package which, when unwrapped, will take you on a journey through the memories and true-life experiences of the people of Corby, from 1930 to the present day.

Telling the story of the coming of Steel to a sleepy Northamptonshire village; the rise and fall of the Industry; the historic battle to Save Our Steel; the struggle to survive as the town rebuilt itself; the doldrums of the Wasted Years; the legacy of Closure; and our dreams and aspirations for the future.

In compiling the book I became aware that we were capturing a very important part of Corby's history, and that the story of the 1980 Steel Strike is often overlooked in the annals of Working Class history.

It is important, as we expand into this new New Town, to remember where we come from. Those moving to the town need to know whom they are coming to live amongst, and that there truly is *More In Corby*, as the website proclaims, than meets the eye (www.moreincorby.co.uk). Our young people need to be able to hold their heads up high, and to kick back at the enduring negative image of Corby.

So if this book captures, remembers, informs, and restores some civic pride, it will have done its Job.

A book, unlike a play, does not need a venue or an audience. It can be taken down off the shelf on a whim, enjoyed alone or shared easily with others, with no need for any intermediary, any technology other than light to see it by.

Contrast that with the transient nature, the impermanence of theatre. Its lure and its frustration is that the hour one *struts and frets...upon the stage* is over all too soon. Witnessed only by the audience that night. And then it is gone.

How often have I been through the letting-go process with a cast who have worked their socks off for months – just for two or three performances? I wonder if it's grief that makes after-show parties so wild and wake-like?

Film sits between the two forms. It attempts to capture fleeting moments for all time.

What actually remains of a play? Emotional memory and internalised imagery. The shared experiences of cast and audience. Sometimes a video or photographs of the performance. A programme as a memento. And the script, now back upon the page – asleep, until someone else reads it out or gives directions to another cast, another time, another place.

So here you have something concrete that you can hold, touch, see and smell. In short...yes, a book...of sorts.

The idea had quite humble origins. It was meant to be a presentation copy of the script for the cast and crew, with photos included. But Kenneth Martin, who joined the project as one of the Photographers at the Arc Theatre, had a wider vision. He suggested that we publish a proper book – this book, full of amazing images.

So, fortified by many a delicious vegetarian lunch, he and I sorted and sifted and placed them until we were satisfied that they did their Job of illustrating the text.

Since this is their purpose in the book, we have deliberately left out detailed captioning. For those who want more information about the photos, I recommend a look at any of the excellent photo books of Corby, where many of these images can be found. Apart from original archive material, we have also included photos of the performances as illustration throughout.

As for the text (expertly and patiently edited by Val Stein), I resurrected the original East Carlton Park script, and included the lyrics to all the songs and the words from any film clips used in the performance.

And so you have in your hands a complete collection of the words and images that have been combined in many ways since July 2006, to tell you the story of the good folk of Corby Town, through the eyes of first its women and then its young people.

It is not really accurate for me to be credited as the sole author of this book. There have been many writers involved. It was important to me that we heard from the generations who have grown up since The Steelworks closed. Emma Boulton Roe wrote the *Wasted Years* section covering 1990-2005. Jack Boulton Roe and Kirsty Graham wrote their own scenes in the *Present Day* sections.

And the *Author's Notes* section contains short pieces of writing from a number of interviewees, as I prefer to let people tell their own stories wherever possible.

One thing print cannot capture is the richness of the voices that told these stories in performance. The cast had a wonderful array of accents: Welsh, Irish and a whole range of Scottish. As both Writer and Director it was very important to me that these regional accents be kept, to reflect authentically what a wonderful mix we have in Corby. However, in the script, only one scene is written down in Glaswegian dialect and only two characters are specified as, respectively, Welsh and Irish.

A note about the capital letters - or *Das Kapital,* as this guiding principle has become known. I made a conscious decision to honour the Workers, their Jobs, the Raw Materials, Tools and Means of Production by giving these, and related words, initial capital letters. The term *Das Kapital* is borrowed appropriately from Karl Marx's treatise of the same name, itself a critical analysis of capitalism, highlighting the exploitation and alienation of Labour.

Once I had made this decision and begun to act on it, I realised that even to me, a Feminist and outspoken Women's Rights Activist, the Work of women was something I took for granted. I spotted Blast-furnaceman, Steelworks, Iron – big, hefty, solid "men's world" things, easy to capitalise. But I failed to notice Cleaner, Canteen Worker and Mop as being equally vital, and therefore worthy of capital letters!

The effect is interesting. Purists will find it annoying. Our Proofreaders certainly found it a challenge! It led to many a discussion and debate. But what it does is emphasise the role of the Worker in this society and make visible what is important in Working Class life.

This principle is discontinued in the *Wasted Years* section in Act Two, to show that from these times onwards the world of Work has irrevocably changed. To be a dispensable worker on the books at one of many agencies, without a fixed employer or contract, is a reality I represent by a return to lower-case. However, in the *Present Day* section, I have developed the concept to include Aspirational Capitals, where young people discuss their future career options, in order to emphasise their innate desire for Proper Jobs.

In addition to the playscript, there is a whole new section, the *Author's Notes*, which is referenced throughout by conventional footnote numbering.

It was not possible to do justice to the many stories I collected during the research when I was writing the play. So I have included them in the *Author's Notes* as "Commentary, Additional Information and More Stories of Steel".

Should you be curious about something which gets barely a mention in the script, and you find a number nearby, follow it to the *Author's Notes* section, where you will find a veritable treasure-chest of explanatory bits and pieces.

For example in *Roots* (Act One Scene 2), we mention Industrial diseases. In the *Author's Notes* you will find a much broader explanation of this topic, with a link to the *Steelworkers' Handbook*.

In the *Wasted Years* section (Act Two Scene 5) the three young women from 1998 choose education, travel or motherhood as their routes. Information about all three choices can be found in the *Notes*.

I did say that this book was a complete collection of the words and images associated with the project. So, to finish there are various miscellaneous items.

The *Creative Process* and *Afterword* explain and ponder the artistic development and transformation of the material from original concept to book.

Cast lists, programmes and other show memorabilia are included, for those of you interested in who did or said what, when, where and why. You will also find the lyrics to all the songs that are not actually in the body of the text, illustrated by photos of the band.

And if you see the name Boulton or Steventon appearing more than once, don't be surprised. I am blessed with being part of a very creative and talented family. Every one of them has contributed to this project. I work with them because they are all very good at what they do.

And without my parents, the late Stanley and Eda Boulton, who moved to Corby in 1955 to open the first Chemist shop, I wouldn't be here. And neither would the Trades and Labour Club, the Maternity Unit, or the Rugby Club - just three of the organisations they helped to establish.

So I dedicate this book to them, and to all those other Comrades who tried to make a difference.

In closing, I hope that *Women of Steel,* the book, is a tribute to the people of Corby, our proud history and our bright, gleaming future.

Paula Boulton
June 2008

# Women of Steel
## a Living History of Corby

## CAST IN ORDER OF APPEARANCE

NARRATOR
IRENE, the Storyteller

GWENDA, a Welsh woman new to Corby, 1934
BRIDIE, her Irish friend
ISA, a Glaswegian widow of a Steelworker, 1960
MAUREEN, a Steelworker from Hartlepool, 1970

Cleaners in the Quantivac, 1960
CISSIE
ELSIE
MARY
MEGAN
SALLY, a new Cleaner
MAVIS, the supervisor

LORRAINE, a young Canteen Worker, 1974

Canteen Workers, 1979
ELAINE
ANNIE
RUBY
JEAN
YVONNE
ISOBEL

KAREN, Union Representative from ISTC (Iron and Steel Trades Confederation)
MAUREEN JOHNSON, Secretary of ROSAC (Retention of Steelmaking at Corby)

Steelworkers from the Save our Steel March
PETER
MONTY

CROWD - Supporters, Demonstrators and March Organisers

MAGGIE THATCHER
BODYGUARDS 1 and 2

PIED PIPER OF WONDERWORLD

Box Factory Workers, 1984
JAN
KAREN
JEAN
ANNIE

JOSIE
ELAINE
YVONNE
ISOBEL

Workers at Corby Clothing Company, 1984
SUSAN
MARGARET
BETTY
LIZZIE
JOY
IRENE
EVELYN

SUPERVISOR
ELLEN, the Union Representative

Young women workers at a chocolate factory in Corby, 1998
JO
EMMA
JEN

STEEL KIDS, twelve young people
YOUNG NARRATOR
DEVELOPER

KIRSTY, a 12-year-old girl

Two 14-year-old friends
PHIL
JEN
PHIL'S INNER VOICE
JEN'S INNER VOICE

18-year-old Hairdressing Students
LEE
JENNIFER

JODIE, Apprentice Mechanic
JORIS, Music Student

Note: For those readers who may wish to use this as a playscript, *Women of Steel* requires a cast of 11-17 women, thirteen young people and three men. There are numerous monologues which can be performed as individual extracts.

I would recommend casting any future production to include as wide a range of regional accents as possible.

ACT ONE

## THE RISE AND FALL OF STEEL
## 1930 - 1979

| | |
|---|---:|
| Prelude to Act One, Song: Village Life | 3 |
| Scene 1: In the Beginning | 7 |
| Song: Jobs May Come | 8 |
| Scene 2: Roots | 9 |
| Scene 3: Homesick, 1934 | 23 |
| Song: Accidents | 27 |
| Scene 4: The Widow, 1960 | 29 |
| Scene 5: One Woman of Steel | 33 |
| Scene 6: Cleaners in the Quantivac, 1960 | 43 |
| Scene 7: A Canteen Worker, Plugmill Canteen, 1974 | 53 |
| Song: As The Works Grows, So the Town Grows | 57 |
| Scene 8: Corby New Town in its Heyday | 65 |
| Scene 9: Union Meeting, Canteen, 1979 | 73 |
| Scene 10: ROSAC Demonstration, London, 28th June 1979 | 89 |
| Song: Keep The Candle Burning | 89 |
| Scene 11: The End of Steel | 93 |

High Street, Corby 1930 showing the Co-op on the right

Hargreaves

Sarringtons

The Nook

PRELUDE TO ACT ONE

SONG: VILLAGE LIFE

*Village life is a pleasure*
*Below us the land, above us the sky*
*Cookie's corner, that's Mr Cook's*
*And the paper shop, now that's Mr Patters'*
*And Nellie Smith will sell you the gobstoppers*
*Don't ever say there's nothing to buy!*
*Sarringtons, Hargreaves and Lees and the Co-op*
*It's only a village but everyone tries*
*It's a small place, yet you can say that*
*Whatever we want, they'll try to supply*

Work there is in Kettering
Or there's the Factory in Cottingham
But it's The Ironworks brings most of the money
A shortage of Jobs was never the cry
Some will go Ploughing and Hoeing and Sowing
They're out in all weathers, the wet and the dry
But The Ironworks are what matter
Without it the village surely would die

Threshing in Weldon at harvest time in the 1890s

*Everyone knows everyone else*
*That's from Mr Payne who lives in the big house*
*To those of us who work in The Works*
*Be you ever so low, or ever so high*
*Meet at the Church or the Scouts or the Hall*
*And with newcomers coming we'll all have to try*
*To be welcoming and whatever*
*We think, we'll do our best to hide*

Village Church

Old Rectory / Hightrees Scouts Centre

High Street

Hay-making

The hedgerows had to be uprooted before Stephenson Way could be built, 1934

## SCENE 1: IN THE BEGINNING

*The stage is bare apart from a table with two chairs, and a projection screen. Enter* NARRATOR.

NARRATOR: Rural England in the 1930s. In the county of Northamptonshire was a small village with an Ironworks providing its main employment. Stewarts and Lloyds decided to build a Steelworks to exploit the rich seam of Iron Ore. But where would the Workers come from? And so began the first wave of migration to Corby. Thousands of men from all over, looking for work… and shortly afterwards their families.

We want to tell you the story of some of those people, how the town rose and fell with The Steelworks, and twenty-five years since Steel, we look at now and the future.

## SONG: JOBS MAY COME

*Jobs may come and Jobs may go*
*But ours they will go on forever*
*Iron and Steel and Tubes we make*
*And if we like you, you can buy some*

*We came to Corby, joined its party*
*Fifty thousand, hale and hearty*
*This is the town that you must see*
*And when you do you'll never leave*
*Mothers, Fathers, Sons and Daughters*
*Stewarts and Lloyds as their employers*
*These Works are the best and we should know*
*For we are the town that made it so*

*We have the Mills, both new and old*
*Whatever we make we get it sold*
*In all the world our Tubes are best*
*We far outsell all of the rest*
*The Tubes we make are there to see*
*They are the highest quality*
*We sell them both home and abroad*
*The whole country it does applaud*

*We have the Ore, it's all around*
*Our whole town it does surround*
*It's turned to Iron then Steel then Coil*
*An institute for moving Oil*
*Praise comes to Corby from near and far*
*When it comes to Steel we are the star*
*In Europe we're the biggest yet*
*We were the first - they won't forget*

## SCENE 2: ROOTS

*Enter IRENE, a cast member, as Storyteller.*

IRENE: Hello. I'm Irene. I want to talk to you about where we Women of Steel came from. I know the story goes that Corby was peopled by Glaswegians… but my dad was from Aberdeen, one of many Fish Workers who moved their families down to Corby in the 50s and 60s.

Irene from Aberdeen

Wooden ships docked at Aberdeen

There was a noticeable Aberdonian community with our own meeting-place, customs and language. We soon fitted in, and, over time, like with any incoming community, we lost some of our distinctiveness.

Mind you, I well remember taking my two bairns back home for the first time. The look on their faces when they heard me talking to the Taxi Driver in the dialect of my childhood! It sounded like a foreign language to them.

Curious bairns

People came to Corby from all over. A real Heinz 57 varieties. Every one of them in search of a Job and a decent house, yet each with their own unique story.

Betty came from Perth in 1956 when her Railwayman father got a Job in The Works.

The family of five lived in a caravan in Burton Latimer at first. A bit of a squeeze when all's said and done. But they settled into their own house in Corby within a year.

Betty from Perth

Betty and her family

A house of your own was one of Corby's biggest attractions. Far better than living in a tenement with four families to a bathroom, or having to live with your parents when you got married.

Josie and her family hailed from Ireland. She grew up in Sussex, spent early married life as an army wife in Germany, and then settled in Corby in 1969.

Josie from Sussex

New Development Corporation houses in the 1950s

On the beach as a child

Then there's Bridie. She visited her brother in Corby in 1960 on the way back to Ireland from New York. She found him settled in a town with a future.

The rest of the family followed shortly afterwards.

Bridie from Ireland

Flying the Emerald Flag in New York

Bridie's family

Corby was a place hard-working people moved to, often from communities with no prospects. There was a growing Irish community, which tended to supply the Labourers who worked to build the town as it grew.

Hard-working people

Labourers[1], Corby 1934

In the 60s, Mass for the Catholics like Bridie living on the Beanfield Estate, was held in St. Brendan's School. A sure way to meet others and keep your culture alive. Eventually they built both a clubhouse and a church.

This pattern was repeated by most of the incoming communities, whatever the religion - as you can see from the number of both clubs and churches across Corby.

The Welfare Club on Occupation Road

Margaret arrived from Aberbargoed in the Welsh Valleys in 1960.

The Aberbargoed bus

Margaret from Wales

Her dad had come here for The Steelworks, along with a good few other Welsh Miners. He was one of the original Bevin Boys[2], conscripted to the Mines during World War II.

Pit-heads at the Coal Mines

He was honest about the Work he'd done before, whereas some of his mates made out that they had the necessary skills. Guess who got the better Jobs?
He already had coal dust in his lungs. Industrial diseases[3] plagued those Working in The Works. Many men were left permanently suffering, or succumbed to early death.

Three Generations of Welsh Miners, 1950

And finally Lorraine, who was born here in Corby. Polish father. Anglo-Italian mother.

A lot of Poles, Latvians and Lithuanians were caught up in the crossfire of World War II and ended up here as displaced persons.

Lorraine from Corby

Remains of Brigstock Camp, first set up in 1939 for POWs and later used to house displaced persons

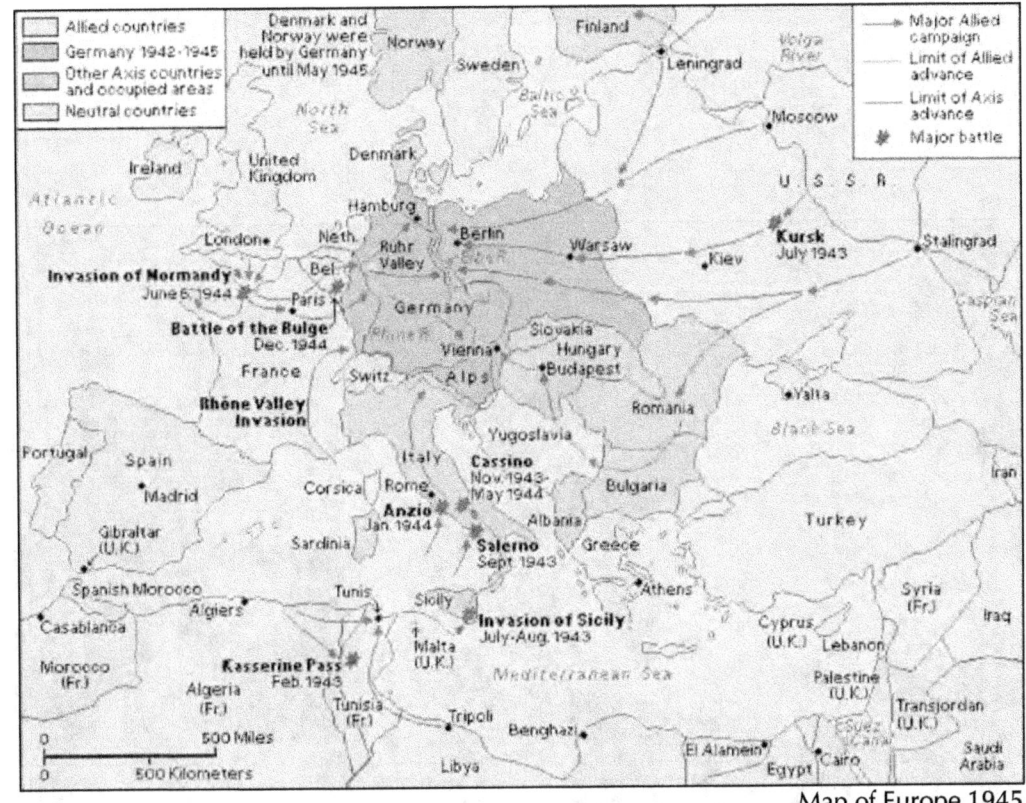

Map of Europe 1945

And of course there were Italian Prisoners of War and American Servicemen, all adding to the ethnic mix that gives Corby its vibrancy.

*She exits.*

Lloyds house living room

## SCENE 3: HOMESICK, 1934

*The table is set to suggest a 1930s Lloyds house living room, complete with a period radio. The sound of a Welsh male voice choir fills the room.*
*GWENDA, a woman from Swansea in her thirties, enters, carrying a box of cutlery, which she sits down at the table to clean. The song on the radio makes her feel homesick.*

*Enter BRIDIE, GWENDA's Irish friend. GWENDA, who is clearly upset, turns off the radio.*

BRIDIE: What's up, Gwenda?

GWENDA: Homesick.

BRIDIE: You'll soon get used to it. Just think about having a house, and a Job, and a future for your family.

23

GWENDA: That's your head talking, and it's my heart that's hurting.

BRIDIE: Tell me then.

GWENDA: Well, I miss my mum and my sisters for a start. They stayed in Swansea and at least they have each other. And the sea, and things to do. And I miss hearing Welsh and speaking Welsh. Don't you miss home?

BRIDIE: Sure I do. We all do. (*Silence.*) I know it seems like a sacrifice now, but just think of your children.

GWENDA: I am doing. Every time I open a drawer or a box of sweets I find these little notes from Carol saying she wants to go home. She misses her friends and hates it at her new school.

BRIDIE: There's not much for them to do here, that's true. And when they do play out, they come in filthy dirty, covered in dust. I can never get my washing clean here. God knows what's in the air!

GWENDA: I know there is Iron. My Robert was collecting Iron Filings off the wall with his magnet. I suppose they'll enjoy the fair though.

BRIDIE: As long as Eamonn remembers to leave the free tickets out!

GWENDA: Is he on nights?[4]

BRIDIE: Why do you think I've come over to you? It's like a bleeding morgue in our house. Creeping around so as not to wake him. I even hung a blanket up at the window cos he says the light keeps him awake. And I dread the kids coming home from school. They need to let off a bit of steam but I'm telling them to *shush* the whole time. And you know I'm up really early so I can sort his feet out before he goes to bed. Those Clogs may keep their feet safe, but they chafe his heels raw.

GWENDA: I worry about my Tom's hearing. You know he forgets he's at home and shouts at me as if I'm deaf. He doesn't even realise he's doing it. And Mr Mitchell next door is the same. I can hear every word he says to Jean. And the rest!

BRIDIE: Is it still bad?

GWENDA: Mostly at the weekend when he's had a drink.

BRIDIE: It's the kids I feel sorry for. I remember my dad doing the same to my mum when I was little. I used to huddle under the bedclothes with my eyes tight shut, willing him to stop it.

GWENDA: She won't talk about it though. Says she fell down the stairs. Anyway listen to me. Do you want a cuppa?

BRIDIE: Sure, I thought you'd never ask. Have you got a biscuit?

GWENDA: You can give me a hand with the veg too. They are the first from Tom's allotment.

*They exit.*

Open Hearth

Bessemer

## SONG: ACCIDENTS

There's fourteen men working on the side of a Furnace
And the gas creeps up on them like some deadly weed
When the only thing to save them has to be brought from London
Can saving only ten men compensate for their greed?

Here the accidents are many, no matter how large or small
When one man has gone there's ten more to take his place
Now Corby has its mortuary, and The Works it helps to fill it
How many years must pass until somebody cares?

The Unions are trying, The Works is getting safer
And mostly we only lose limbs instead of lives
But what about the ghost shift who will never leave here
Will they wander the site long after we've gone?

Skimming Ladles

Blast-furnace

## SCENE 4: THE WIDOW, 1960

*Enter* ISA, *a Glaswegian woman in her forties, who sits down at the empty table and looks through a photo album.*

ISA: That's Erchie, ma man.
We'd 'a been married twenty-five years the morra. We came tae Corby fae Gleasga[5] when they shut doon the Works up there. They sed they needed people fur the Joabs. Why they couldnae 'ave just built the new Works up in Scotland is a mystery tae me.

But naw - move the people doon tae another country, thousands o' us. Men first, and then the wimmen and wains. What a bloody upheaval.

Living wi'oot yer man, bringing up yer wains on yer ain while he was doon here in a camp wi' the rest of the men. Nothin' tae dae but drink and fight wi'oot us wimmen tae keep them in order. No' that they didnae deserve a dram after a hard day's Graft in that hell-hole. The stories ma Erchie used tae tell me. The heat. The thirst. The noise. The accidents!

Well that's how I lost ma Erchie. He was wan o' the men that fell into the Molten Steel[6] when the planks gave way.

Steelworker "Tapping"

Health and safety? They didnae have safety precautions in them days! They didnae care, men were ten a penny. Oh, I got a nice letter from Stewarts and Lloyds when he died. But that and the wee drap compensation couldnae replace a faithir or gi' me back ma man.

Oh aye, The Works wis guid tae him in many ways. A steady Joab wi' a future. Highest-paid Work you could find roon here. And he had the best bunch o' pals onywan could ask fur. They wur there fur me an ma wains efter the accident. But then the whole toon is like that - I suppose we're just wan big clan!

Nae matter where you came fae, you'd left a lot behind. Family, friends, yer ain hoose, a familiar way of life, even a language. There're enough Scots here to make ye forget that this is England sometimes. But you know, up the road no-one ever asks me to slow doon cos they cannae understand whit I'm sayin'! Why don't I go back? Well, there's nae future fur the wains. Nae Joabs. At least here they'll hae Work. Ma Rab's in the Tubes, and when Alec, ma next eldest, finishes school next year he'll be straight doon The Works. Tae begin wi' he'll be getting a boy's wage. It willnae be till he turns twenty-wan that he gets a man's money, but at least it's another wage comin' in.

Ma Fiona will be next. Oh aye, she'll hae a choice. No' jis the Offices or Cleaning! Wimmen work on the Shoap Flare as well y'know. Mind you, if she cerries on the way she is wi' that young Jamie, she'll be sterting a family before a Joab. Just think! Me... a Granny! I'm no' ready fur that! (ISA *looks fondly at the photograph of Erchie.*) We used tae talk aboot growin auld thegether. Now he'll never see his granwains.

Aye... an' it'll be sad fur them no tae hae a grampa. Still! Their life will be so different, a lot easier tae oors. She better no' be expectin' me tae look after they wains. I've got ma own life tae lead noo!

Listen tae me bletherin' on. I've things tae dae. Nice talking tae ye. Cheery bye!

*She exits.*

Rivers of Steel

Steelworker "surrounded" by Molten Steel

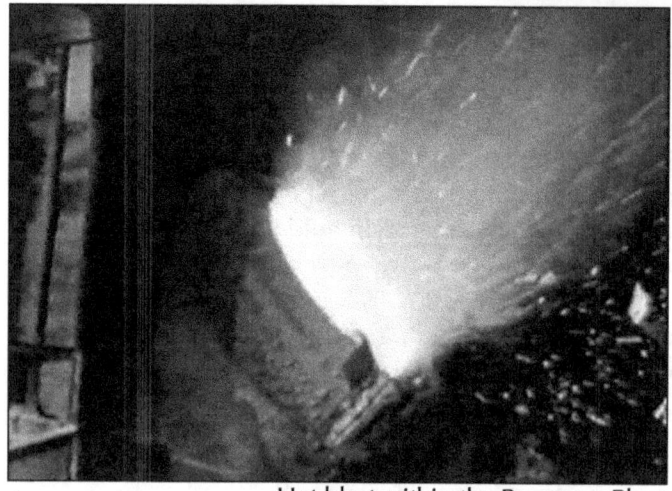
Hot blast within the Bessemer Plant

## SCENE 5: ONE WOMAN OF STEEL

*Enter MAUREEN. The table has been re-set as her kitchen in the 1970s. Recorded sounds from inside a Steelworks accompany the image of a woman Steelworker.*

MAUREEN: I was the youngest woman in the Steelworks[7] in Hartlepool. Twenty-four, I was. My Job was Tally-woman. I used to have to lean over and mark the white-hot Steel as it came out. I never had any hair at the front of my head cos I didn't like to keep the protective cap down over my eyes. Silly when I think of it now, but back then I had my looks to consider.

I was the last woman to leave too. We women were all being paid off, like after the war. Training up the lads, we were. They were even cheaper than us to employ.

Anyway how did I come to Corby? My husband applied to be a Fuel Technologist at Stewarts and Lloyds, and the first I ever heard mention of the place was when he told me he was going for an interview.

Stewarts and Lloyds Steelworks

He got the Job and we came down in 1965. We were offered a staff house at East Carlton Park.

You like them? I'd have gone stir-crazy living out in the sticks. No! I was a townie, so we went for one of the new staff houses on the Lincoln.

The original staff hostel

Lincoln Way when it was first built

Yes, you heard me right! From Sower Leys to Grantham Walk were all staff houses. Snob Hill they called it. Oh, it was state-of-the-art then, I can tell you. The architect won awards and all sorts! "How many women can you condemn to a life of misery?" awards! Each of us in solitary confinement, never seeing another soul from day to day. No doorstep culture or over-the-fence chat… you'd have needed a bloody ladder for that. Six-foot-high fences out the back.

Six-foot-high fences, erected to give some "privacy"

I used to sit at my door for hours hoping someone would pass by. No-one ever did. There was nothing to do.

I went to my doctor's, I was that depressed. "Oh!" he said, "the Valium Estate," and handed over a prescription. Later they called it "the Lincoln Blues."

Back home me and my mum had been in a ladies' club. So I got to thinking that we needed something like that here. The Council gave us a bungalow on Lincoln Way...

Lincoln Way

...and soon there were two full days of activities each week. It wasn't until us women got talking that we realised we were all in the same boat. Not just the isolation, but the lack of facilities... the long haul to the town and back, and the school stuck out in the middle of a field like the Lone Ranger.

So we did something about it. Once we got started, there was no stopping us. We outgrew the bungalow, so the Council gave us two shop units on Canada Square.

Shop units on Canada Square

Soon we had play groups and one o'clock clubs as well as our social activities, and after three years it became a licensed club. I left the estate for a short time... but I missed it. Missed the sense of community we'd created.

Canada Square in the early 1970s

I missed the woods and the lack of traffic. So I moved back.

Kingswood

I've seen it go through some changes. The Golden Cockerel...

Lincoln Square

...to The Lincoln.

From The Maple Leaf, to The Square Peg, to The Leaf. From the day the Canadian High Commissioner came to open Canada Square...

...to the knocking down of the houses on Lincoln Way.

Oh yes, "the Valium Estate," the worst estate.

But I've raised my family here, it's where I live, it's my home.[8]

*Exit* MAUREEN.

## SCENE 6: CLEANERS IN THE QUANTIVAC, 1960

*Enter* ELSIE, *a Cleaner, who watches a short extract from a 1960s promotional film, "Double Harvest", made by Stewarts and Lloyds. During the film, she re-sets the table as office furniture.*

FILM PRESENTER: At first impression it would seem the fairer sex has no place in this world of men. In fact, women are playing an increasingly important role in this, as in so many other branches of Industry.

Secretary

Secretaries and Shorthand Typists, upon whom so much of the mechanics of business depend, are taken almost for granted.

Shorthand Typist

But there are many more examples of the female contribution. The manipulation of modern equipment for Data Processing and the like requires a dexterity and Skill which women seem particularly quick to learn.

Data Processor

Dexterity and Skill

Technical Diagram Tracer

Their temperament is well-suited to the intricacies of Technical Diagram Tracing.

There are a number of medical centres within the Plant, and this one in the Tubeworks is a fine example of the facilities provided.

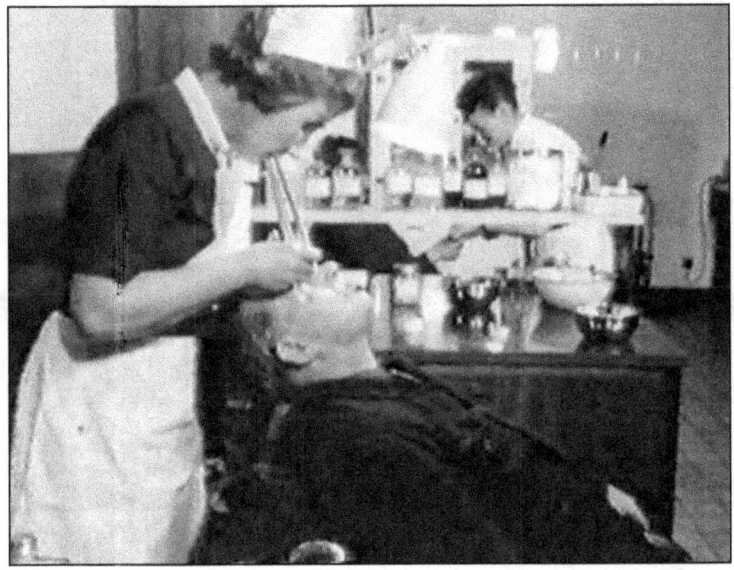

Nurse

Here, as always, of course, woman is indispensable. In a Job of this kind, minor injuries are inevitable and relatively routine. The general medical check-ups and the services of resident Doctors are available to all.

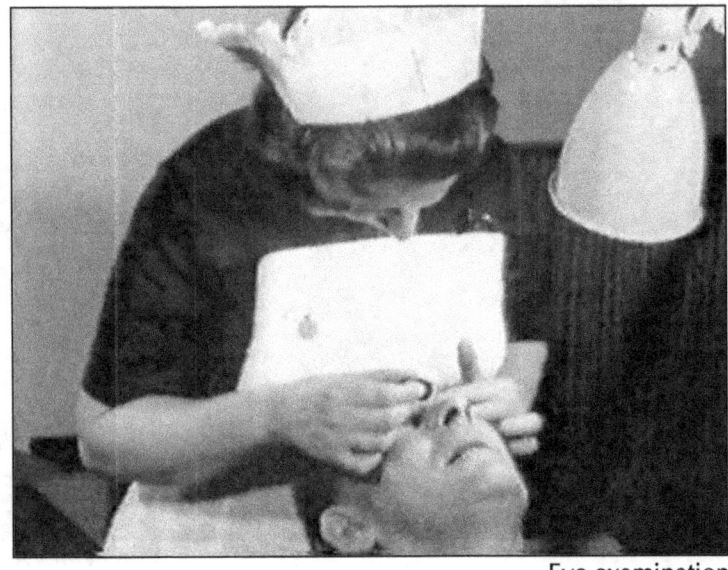

Eye examination

Modern Canteen

The old days of working through and grabbing a bite wherever possible are no more. Today the men can feed and relax in a modern Canteen.

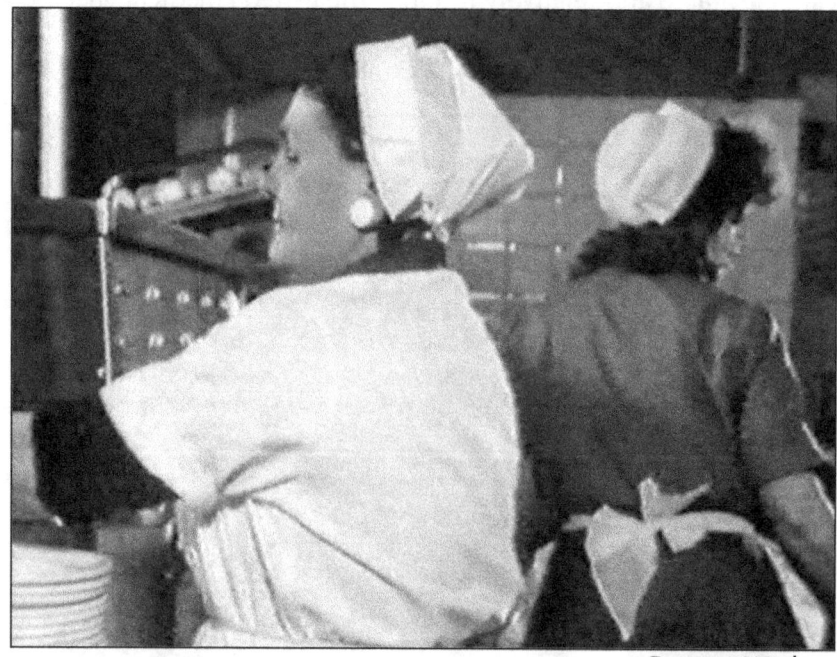

Canteen Workers

What a place to clean!

ELSIE: Aye, we women did lots of Jobs down The Works. All those, and on the Shop Floor too. Now me... I was one of an army of Cleaners. Ever wondered what happened once the boss went home?

ELSIE *starts Mopping the floor. Enter* CISSIE, *another Cleaner, who joins in. They work in companiable silence for a while.*

ELSIE: I saw Maggie earlier on. She's the size of a house. I reckon she's carrying a boy. It's all at the front.

CISSIE: She's lucky to have her mum down here. When I had my first I was alone. Didn't have a clue.

ELSIE: We had that long drive over to Kettering too. At least now there is the Maternity Unit.

CISSIE: Thank goodness for that. My cousin lost one of her twins back in 1947. Remember that really cold winter? The roads were all snowed up and by the time they got to the hospital the baby was dead.

*Enter MARY, another Cleaner.*

MARY: It's freezing out there. Get the kettle on!

ELSIE: I've already made it.

CISSIE: Would you not be better doing a bit of Work first?

MARY: Oh, I'll get started when me hands are warmed through.

ELSIE: Well if you're having tea, I suppose we could join you.

CISSIE: I'm sure the boss is off home anyway.

MARY: You know there was a new lass on the bus sitting in my seat! Cheek of it!

ELSIE *(to MARY)*: Have you put your money in for Maggie?

MARY: Not yet, but I'll give it you next week, I promise. Money's a bit tight this week. What did you get her anyway?

ELSIE: A house-coat, like we said... out of the catalogue.

*SALLY, a new employee, appears in the doorway.*

SALLY: Is this the Quantivac?

CISSIE: Aye it is, lass. Come in, we don't bite. Are you new?

*SALLY nods her head and hesitantly enters.*

MARY: You're a bit late, aren't you?

SALLY: I went to the wrong place!

MARY: How come?

SALLY: Well, me dad said to just follow the men. So I did... right into the blooming showers. This one man kindly brought me here in his truck.

*Enter MAVIS, the Supervisor.*

MAVIS: So, are you lot coming or going?

MARY: Coming!

ELSIE: Going!

CISSIE: Gone!

MAVIS *(strolling to shelves and checking for dust):* I sincerely hope you intend to do some Work this evening? Perhaps you plan to stay later instead, to make up for starting late? *(She exits, slamming the door.)*

MARY: I'd best get started. *(To Sally):* Are you coming with me? I'll show you the ropes. *(To the others):* See you later.

*Exit MARY and SALLY.*

ELSIE *(handing her cup to CISSIE):* Read my tea-leaves before I rinse my cup.

CISSIE *(after gazing at the leaves for a while):* Well, I see a bit of a row between you and someone small.

ELSIE: Me! I never fall out with anyone. *(Waits.)* Is that all? Best keep reading that book your daughter got you. *(She sets to Mopping the floor.)* You know I still do my floors on my hands and knees. I'd love a Mop Bucket like this. Maybe Santa will remember me at Christmas.

CISSIE: There's one out in the yard.

ELSIE: Yes, I've seen it.

CISSIE: Well, take it home with you!

ELSIE: Oh, I couldn't steal it!

CISSIE: It wouldn't be theft... it's been out there for ages.

ELSIE: Well, how would I clock out with that in my hands?

CISSIE: Oh, I'll clock you out... I'll meet you outside tomorrow.

ELSIE: Would you really? That's awful kind of you. I'll have to walk home though. It would be snowing. Just my luck.

*Enter MARY and SALLY.*

MARY: Well that's me finished. I'm off down the Canteen for some chips. See you tomorrow. *(She hangs up her dirty Mop and exits.)*

CISSIE: I'm glad I don't have to eat at her table if her home's as clatty as she is!

ELSIE: Ach! She means well. *(To SALLY)*: Don't do what she does, love - rinse your Mop out in clean water before you finish.

*Enter MEGAN, another Cleaner.*

MEGAN: Hello, are you all still here? *(She starts unloading a large bag of washing and draping it on the radiators.)* Bloody Spin-Dryer broke and I'll never get this all dried in this weather.

CISSIE: Big Mavis is on the war-path!

MEGAN: Oh Christ, I thought she'd have gone home by now.

CISSIE *and* ELSIE: So did we!

MEGAN: Well, sod it! I'm sure she's seen a man's long-johns before. I'm Cleaning over at the Coke Ovens anyway, so if I'm not here she won't know whose they are, will she? *(She wipes her hands on her Pinny and exits in a hurry. The others get ready to leave.)*

CISSIE: Rather her than me!

ELSIE *(to* SALLY*):* Are you coming with us, lass? We'll show you where to go... avoiding the showers!

CISSIE *(to* ELSIE*):* Aren't you forgetting your Bucket?

ELSIE: Oh yes... I'll get it now. See you tomorrow. *(She exits.)*

CISSIE: She'll be changing her name to Liza by tomorrow - that Bucket's full of holes!

*They exit laughing and singing the song "There's a hole in my Bucket".*

Works Canteen

## SCENE 7: A CANTEEN WORKER, PLUGMILL CANTEEN, 1974

*Enter LORRAINE, a young Canteen Worker, Sweeping the floor with a Broom.*

LORRAINE *(to audience):* Do you know - I've only been working here for six months. But it feels a lot longer. Came straight from school.

Why the Plugmill Canteen? Well… I'd failed my "A" levels. One mate did well and was off to uni. I'd just been to my other friend's wedding and I knew I wasn't ready for that! So, I applied for a Job as Assistant Cook down here at The Works. I thought it'd be a doddle! How wrong can you be? It is heavy Work - and I mean heavy. I suppose I just hadn't thought about the size of everything on an Industrial scale. This is just one of many Canteens - Staff and Works.

Anyway, cos I'm strong, I get quite a lot of the lifting to do. I am on Six to Two and Two to Ten. I hate Two to Ten. It feels like a waste of a day. Whilst Six to Two suits me just fine. Many's the time I watch the sunrise on my way down Sower Leys Road after a cracking all-night party up the Lincoln somewhere. I drop in at home and then carry on straight down to The Works. Over the flyover, clocking in on the dot of six! Still in my fur coat, mind, and often with a hangover. I'm sure at the start the older women wondered who I thought I was, swanning around in that.

Anyway, handling twenty-four eggs at a time with a hangover is no mean feat, I can tell you! And the Toaster - I have rows of burn marks on my arms from the Grill. It's the breakfasts I do most. Egg and Bacon Double-Decker. Sausage, Egg and Bacon Double-Decker. Egg and Sausage Double-Decker - all on toast. Big men... big appetites... lots of toast!

That's not all we serve. Pie and Chips, grey Cabbage, Mashed Potato by the bathful. Lottie's Homemade Soup - and puddings. Apple Crumble and Custard - gallons of the stuff. Dropping a huge vat of that into the hot water without trapping your fingers is quite an art, I can tell you.

But then there is a lot of Skill involved in this Job. I've learned how to Wring out a Dishcloth properly and how to Mop floors. They are so greasy they need soaked first. The older women showed me. They are really helpful - and there's some right characters.

Workers in the Canteen enjoying a social[9]

Lottie … singing away with the Dishcloth tails in her Pinny. Norah Sweeney, with her hair all yellow at the front from the nicotine. Peggy… stuck in that wee Kiosk Selling cigarettes, sweets, matches. It's no bigger than a tiny cupboard. And Florence Winstanley. Fifty-five. The Chip Fryer. She gave me a lovely garnet ring for helping her with the chips.

Sometimes I have to Count the money in the vending machines, or I go on the Tills. That's my favourite Job. The men send down the Apprentices with a big box to get their food. They come themselves if it's overtime. The line is really long, and the meal is free. I take names then, not money. You'd be surprised the number of men with fingers missing.

I met my boyfriend here. He's an Apprentice. He'd often sit on his own, and sometimes I'd sneak into the Kiosk so I could look at him without him noticing. Dark and mysterious… I also work part-time as a Barmaid up The Domino. One night he came in and we started talking.

I knew I didn't want to spend my life Frying eggs - however good the company. Not that I'm afraid of hard Work. But I want to see more of the world. So him and me are off hitching to the south of France. I got my passport the other week. It was when I wrote "Assistant Cook" that I decided I wanted more. Next time, I'll write "Photographer!"

*She exits.*

## SONG: AS THE WORKS GROWS, SO THE TOWN GROWS[10]

*From cities and the Industries*
*From Scotland they came*
*They all arrived at Kettering*
*Having travelled down by train*
*Then to Corby on another train*
*No-one would go by bus*
*They're unreliable, undependable*
*Not even worth a cuss*

*There is nothing here, nothing to do*
*Nowhere to go or play*
*There are no roads, there are no lights*
*And nowhere to pray*
*No tenements, no corner shops*
*Just pubs to drink your fill*
*And miles of fields and open space*
*With plenty time to kill*

*Chorus: As The Works grows
So the town grows
One relying on the other
And if one dies, they both die
Just as if they had been lovers*

*The houses down in Stevie Way
Have gardens to be dug
It's the first time for many
It could become a drug
For in Scotland there's no garden
No room, just discontent
And now there's mouths to feed and things to grow
We need an allotment*

*Down in Bessemer and Kelvin Grove*
*The houses they appear*
*Also East Carlton where the staff live*
*The difference it is clear*
*We have the pubs to enjoy ourselves*
*But still nowhere to pray*
*What we need now are some churches*
*This means we're here to stay*

*Chorus*

Church of Scotland

*The Catholic Church now's established*
*It's going to expand*
*And the Scots have raised six thousand pounds*
*Their church it will be grand*
*But the Baptist and Congregational Church*
*They still have far to go*
*So they'll meet in Messrs Lloyds Cinema*
*But they're biding time, you know*

*With the churches, houses, graveyards too*
*The town it has been born*
*With the Scots in the majority*
*It didn't take them long*
*For if you come from Stevie Way*
*It's just like being home*
*Now you live in Little Scotland*
*There is no need to roam!*

*Instrumental: Scottish fiddle music, "Cock of the North".*

*During this tune, a series of images from the Highland Gathering appears on the screen (overleaf).*

Corporation Street before pedestrianisation

## SCENE 8: CORBY NEW TOWN IN ITS HEYDAY

*This purely visual scene[11] consists of a series of images depicting Corby New Town as a thriving and bustling community. As it says in "Double Harvest" - a 1960s promotional film made by Stewarts and Lloyds:*

FILM PRESENTER: Production in The Works goes on round the clock. Round the clock too is the Job of those who provide relaxation in Corby. Just as continuous as production at The Plant is the demand for diversion. Meeting much of this demand is the company's Recreation Club and the many facilities provided within its twenty-acre grounds.

But recreation need no longer be confined to the club. The many interests of a mixed population have created an unusually varied social life for so young a town.

Clubs and societies of every description are keenly supported as well as the more obvious sporting activities.

Priors Hall Golf Course

Snooker Hall

Corby Bowling

Stewarts and Lloyds Lawn Bowls Club

50-metre swimming pool

Festival Hall The lounge of S & L Welfare Club

Drinking up in The Pluto The Nag's Head

Market Square

Co-operative Department Store

Post Office, Rockingham Road

Queens Square, showing *Spirit of Corby* Sculpture

View from The Strathclyde Hotel looking back to The Steelworks

SCENE 9: UNION MEETING, CANTEEN, 1979

*The stage is now set as a Canteen. Enter NARRATOR.*

NARRATOR: In February 1979, British Steel announced plans to close the Steel end of The Corby Plant[12], with the potential loss of 5,500 Jobs. By April that figure was estimated at 12,000. The newly-formed campaign group ROSAC[13] - Retention of Steelmaking at Corby - spearheaded the fight to Save Steel, alongside the ISTC and other Trade Unions.

*Enter a group of Canteen Staff – ELAINE, ANNIE, RUBY, JEAN, YVONNE and ISOBEL. They gather round the table.*

ELAINE: What's this meeting about then?

ANNIE: Closure, no doubt.

RUBY: My man says that's not gonna happen cos the Union's not said anything official yet.

JEAN: When are people gonna wake up? Why are we up and down to London and holding Meetings and Actions if there is no threat?

RUBY: Left-wing troublemakers, the lot of you!

ANNIE: I was on the last coach to London and I'm no troublemaker. This town relies on The Works, and without it there's no future for my kids.

RUBY: Talking of troublemakers… *(She exits, in a huff.)*

*Enter KAREN, the Union Representative.*

ALL: Hello.

KAREN: As the ISTC Rep, I'm here to explain that we want your support for a National Strike to improve Wages throughout the Steel Industry. I'm counting on you to come out and make this a solid response.

JEAN: Where has the Union been while I've been freezing my arse off on the ROSAC stall on a Saturday?

KAREN: This isn't about Closures, ladies, this is about Wages.

JEAN: What bloody good is a Wage rise if you haven't got a Job?

KAREN: I agree we need to keep on with our own Campaign, but this is about the Steel Industry nationally. And the Tubeworks is not under threat! We need to stand with them.

YVONNE: They didn't stand with us, did they? All the men thought about when we were out on Strike was their sodding stomachs. They didn't take us seriously at all.

ISOBEL: I'll do what my man thinks best… The Blast-furnacemen reckon we should be accepting Closure and already talking about the money.

ELAINE: I've got a son in the Tubes and a husband in the Coke Ovens. Which way do I go?

ISOBEL: Well, my man heard that they'll lose any offer on the table if they come out.

KAREN: BSC scaremongering. The Redundancy settlement is a separate issue. We've got to think about the future.

JEAN: There isn't one if The Works shuts!

YVONNE: If my husband and I both Strike now, we'll have nothing to live off and no Job at the end of it. And I for one have a mortgage to pay for, and we've families to feed.

ANNIE: Well I've never crossed a Picket Line in my life and I don't intend to start now. OK, The Works may be closing, but let's go out with a bang and show Maggie the Milk Snatcher how much the country relies on Steel.

KAREN: Well said! It'll be the Miners next if she has her way. Mark my words. So ladies, all those in favour of supporting the Strike…[14]

*This gets a very lukewarm response from the Canteen Staff. They exit, muttering.*

KAREN *(to audience):* Of course when we first heard about Closures we all stood together. We knew that there would be no future for the town and for our kids. And we thought we could fight it.

Protest meeting with Jimmy Reid

*Enter MAUREEN JOHNSON, the ROSAC Secretary.*

MAUREEN: We lobbied BSC wherever we could find them.

Protest at Graham House

There were coaches went down to meet the men who walked to London to hand in the Petition. Corby's own Jarrow-style March.

Marching down Park Lane, London

There were numerous local Protests and we had Days of Action.

KAREN: There was no need to persuade and cajole Workers to Strike in the September of 1979 when it was decided to bring the whole town to a halt. The Walk-out here at The Works was solid.

The mass Walk-out at The Works, 20th September 1979

MAUREEN: The community was right there behind us. Schools brought their students along, and mums with babies in prams and pushchairs joined the March.

KAREN: Young and old united in the simple knowledge that without its heart of Steel our town would die.

Children fighting for their future

MAUREEN: The Chamber of Commerce agreed to close down the town. Nothing moved! Nothing opened!

*Overleaf:* The impressive turnout in West Glebe Park

We reckon it was the first time anything like that had happened in this country. A whole town united in defence of its future.

KAREN: And we weren't alone. Local Unions, like the Post Office Workers and the Shop Workers, came out in support. And Miners, Dockers, Car Workers and Steelworkers from other towns all came to Corby to show their solidarity.

MAUREEN: They knew that if the Closures went ahead in Corby, it was a case of "who was next in line?"

Note the SOS on the Gasometer

KAREN: The police were on red alert.

Demonstration in Everest Lane Car Park, Corby

Unnecessary police presence

Remember this was 1979, before Greenham Common and the Miners' Strike. Before police in riot gear[15] were a common sight.

For the Union Reps to get into the meeting with British Steel, they had to get through a cordon of police four deep.

The police cordon at BSC Headquarters

MAUREEN: They needn't have worried. A whole town out on the streets and no trouble.

Exciting times.

KAREN: What was it like?

MAUREEN: We'll show you.

Steelworkers protesting outside the Festival Hall

The Corby to London Save Our Steel March leaving the Civic Centre, June 1979

The March arriving in London

SCENE 10: ROSAC DEMONSTRATION,
LONDON, 28TH JUNE 1979

KAREN *and* MAUREEN *remain on stage and turn the table into a ROSAC Campaign stall. The cast enter as Supporters and Organisers from Corby, who have just arrived in London to greet the Steelworkers who marched to London with the Save Our Steel Petition. They are carrying homemade Placards and Banners – including the original ROSAC Banner.*

SONG: KEEP THE CANDLE BURNING
(written to raise funds for the ROSAC Campaign by Mike Carver)

*Stewarts and Lloyds came down here to drag the Iron Ore*
*Workers came from Glasgow through Corby's open door*
*BSC took over and said we were secure*
*Now we're for the scrap heap - they don't need us any more*
*Have you heard of Corby? It's the future, a new town*
*Have you heard of Corby? Now they're trying to close it down*
*Years ago we came here - a good Job, a home our goal*
*The ads forgot to mention that we'd end up on the dole*

Keep the Candle burning
Keep the town alive
Keep the Drag Lines walking
Let the town survive

We could have been assembling Volkswagens by the score
But the government wouldn't let them in
Said Steel needs you much more
Smooth forked-tongued industrial vandals
Sponsored by the state
Condemn you like an old tin can to the dustbin out the gate

The story the world over's just the same
Workers victimised in Pittsburgh, Shotton and Lorraine
No crime, no charge, no court, no trial but wait
Just prosecution, no defence, but an execution date

Keep the Candle burning
Keep the town alive
Keep the Drag Lines walking
Let the town survive

We defy you to close The Steelworks down
We defy you, you can't murder this our town
BSC and tory government - we don't need you around
We defy you, we won't let you steal our town

We'll send out Flying Pickets
We'll Strike, don't be perplexed
Other Plants will give support
When we tell them they'll be next
If you live in Corby, BSC give you the dole
Out with useless bosses - let the Workers take control!

Keep the Candle burning
Keep the town alive
Keep the Drag Lines walking
Let the town survive

*Enter* MONTY *and* PETER, *two Steelworkers. The Demonstration Organisers greet them warmly, take them to meet the crowd, and eventually guide them over to the podium.*

ORGANISER: I'd like to introduce our first speaker - Peter McGowan!

PETER: At the end of this long and memorable March, I would like to pay tribute to the Corby public for their long and loyal support during the campaign to Save Our Steelworks.

I would also like to take this opportunity to thank you on behalf of ROSAC and the Marchers for coming here today, to demonstrate to the members of parliament our total opposition to the Closure plans and the effect it will have on the town and its people.

I would also like to express our sincere gratitude for the very kind gestures of hospitality we received during our long walk from Trades Councils and the people of Irthlingborough, Rushden, Bedford, Luton, Dunstable, St Albans, and Brent, who made us very welcome, especially the Luton Fire and Paramedic Services who even arranged medical check-ups at a local hospital for us.

Our final challenge is now to meet and present on your behalf this Petition to the members of parliament, in the hope that they will recognise that their decision will be catastrophic for Corby.

Let's raise the battle cry, let the politicians know that the Corby people are on their doorstep!

Save Steel! Save Corby!
Save Steel! Save Corby!

*The crowd react very supportively.*

The ROSAC Banner

## SCENE 11: THE END OF STEEL

*This scene is an unbroken continuation from Scene 10, with everyone remaining in place.*

*Enter MAGGIE THATCHER with her bodyguards, who are carrying a detonator. The crowd reacts with hostility.*

MONTY: What are you doing here? Why don't you get back to Grantham and sell some more beans, you old fart?

*The tension dissolves as the crowd laugh.*

MAGGIE: Thank you for that warm welcome! This is the first demonstration I have ever been on - and I assure you it will be my last. *(Aside):* And theirs too, if I have my way.

MONTY: We never asked you to come!

MAGGIE: What is all this shouting and yelling and placard-waving going to achieve?

MONTY: Publicity!

MAGGIE: Do you think we take a blind bit of notice? Of course we don't!

MONTY: We've noticed!

MAGGIE: But we do care.

CROWD: Rubbish!

MAGGIE: Steel is dead. Who wants to work in heavy industry?[16]

CROWD: We do!

MAGGIE: We can leave that to men overseas and import what we need.

MONTY: What's wrong with BRITISH Steel?

CROWD *(chanting)*: Save Our Steel! Save Our Steel!

MAGGIE: We promise to find you new jobs - clean jobs, flexible jobs.

CROWD *(shouting, amid general pandemonium)*: We want the ones we've got! *(and other ad lib responses.)*

MAGGIE: *(watching, unmoved)*: Oh, so you're not convinced?

CROWD: NO!

MAGGIE: You say you'll keep on fighting?

CROWD: YES!

MAGGIE: Very stirring stuff… but YOU voted for me and my Government.

CROWD: Oh, no, we didn't!

MAGGIE: Oh, yes, you did! So let's get rid of these dinosaurs… finish the work of my predecessors - the labour government! Make way for the future!

SOUNDTRACK: *The 1812 Overture, played very loudly.*

MAGGIE: Five… Four… Three… Two… One!

CROWD *(chanting loudly during MAGGIE's countdown)*: Save Our Steel! Maggie! Maggie! Maggie! Out! Out! Out! *(and other ad lib responses.)*

*As MAGGIE counts down to demolition, newspaper headlines referring to the battle to save The Steelworks appear one after another on the screen, fast-forwarding through time.*

## PROPHETS OF DOOM

## Industrial action planned by steel union over Corby

## Corby to be made a development area

*Then MAGGIE presses the detonator repeatedly, in time with the sound of cannon fire on the soundtrack, synchronised with images on the screen detailing the demolition[17] of The Steelworks.*

MONTY *angrily makes as if to leave the stage. He tries to encourage* PETER *to go with him, but* PETER *is overwhelmed by the pointless destruction and is sitting dejectedly holding his Steel Hat in his hands.*

MONTY *(walking offstage)*: You'll not get away with this! We'll keep fighting!

*The crowd are devastated, their Placards drooping. There is a stunned silence. For the time being* MAGGIE *has won. It is important to let the audience really feel the dejection and desolation - to experience the irreparable damage to the community.*

*The 1812 Overture finishes. There is silence.*

MAGGIE: So, don't just stand there! Off to the dole queue, all of you. You'll soon find another job!

*All exit.*

## ACT TWO

### WONDERWORLD, WONDERWHEN?
### 1984

| | |
|---|---|
| Prelude to Act Two, Song: WonderWorld | 103 |
| Scene 1: Enterprise Zone | 105 |
| Scene 2: Broken Dreams | 109 |
| Song: Broken Dreams | 111 |
| Scene 3: The Aftermath | 113 |
| Scene 4: Stand Your Ground | 129 |
| Song: Sweatshop | 130 |
| Song: WonderWorld (Reprise) | 138 |

### WASTED YEARS
### 1990 - 2005

| | |
|---|---|
| Scene 5: A chocolate factory in Corby 1998 *by Emma Boulton Roe* | 139 |

### THE PRESENT DAY

| | |
|---|---|
| Scene 6: Steel Kids | 153 |
| Scene 7: The Future | 159 |
| Scene 8: I Wish *by Kirsty Graham* | 167 |
| Scene 9: 'Til the End *by Jack Boulton Roe* | 170 |
| Scene 10: A Cut Above | 175 |
| Scene 11: Hope for the Future | 181 |
| Song: Give Us a Job to Do in Corby | 183 |

Environment Secretary Kenneth Baker officially opens Steel Road in 1985

PRELUDE TO ACT TWO

SONG: WONDERWORLD

*There's a green field not far away*
*Outside of our town wall*
*Some say it will give us ten thousand Jobs*
*We say it's a load of balls!*
*For fifteen years it's been a field*
*And as you see nothing has changed*
*If you can see a theme park there*
*God, you must be deranged!*

*In 1980 The Steelworks closed*
*Eight thousand were on the dole*
*The council got some whizz-kids in*
*They said we can fill that hole*
*So the plans were made, the money was spent*
*Everything was going to be fine*
*But here we are nearly ten years on*
*And all we've got is a 40-foot sign*
*Saying –*

*Welcome to WonderWorld*
*Welcome to WonderWorld*
*Welcome to WonderWorld*
*Welcome to WonderWorld*

*The backers came and went, the years went by*
*Still nothing can be seen*
*The Telegraph mentioned it now and again*
*We thought it was all a dream*
*Now near local election time*
*More money has been found*
*But do you want to bet how long it takes*
*Before they start digging the ground?*
*So –*

*Welcome to WonderWorld*
*Welcome to WonderWorld*
*Welcome to WonderWorld*
*Welcome to WonderWorld*

*The Chase Manhattan Banks arrived*
*More money than we need*
*But still we'd like to see their cash*
*Or is it just our greed?*
*We thought the Jobs would help us here*
*We thought they would help the town*
*But the backers keep doing what they are best at*
*The backers keep backing down*

*Welcome to WonderWorld*
*Welcome to WonderWorld*
*Welcome to WonderWorld*
*Welcome to WonderWorld*

## SCENE 1: ENTERPRISE ZONE

*The* PIED PIPER OF WONDERWORLD, *a character based on Michael Heseltine and the Pied Piper of Hamelin, enters in front of closed curtains.*

PIED PIPER:  Why so glum? I'm your chum
　　　　　　Come with me, you will see
　　　　　　From the ashes you will rise
　　　　　　Like a phoenix, and you'll thrive
　　　　　　Lots of new Jobs, clean and smart
　　　　　　Women now can play their part
　　　　　　Enterprise, that's where it's at –
　　　　　　Or Maggie dear will eat her hat!

*Enter* MAGGIE THATCHER *and two* BODYGUARDS. *Between them they perform a ribbon-cutting ceremony. They exit.*

*The curtains open to reveal a row of chairs representing a Conveyor Belt. A film about WonderWorld is playing on the screen.*

FILM PRESENTER: This is WonderWorld, a £367 million leisure project which its backers say will provide 3,000 Jobs. It has received the personal support of Mrs Thatcher.

Group 5, the developers, promise a unique family day out. An all-year-round combination of Disney-style theme park and nursery-rhyme fantasy. But WonderWorld has seen deadlines come and go, and it remains a plastic model.

With the depression still biting deep, more women are looking for Work. Many of Corby's new Jobs have gone to them and not the ex-Steelworkers.

EX-STEELWORKER: I've been up and down here for years now, trying to look for a Job, and I haven't found one yet.

INTERVIEWER: Is it difficult for someone like you to get a Job?

EX-STEELWORKER: I don't think I'll ever Work again, to tell you the truth.

*Film clip ends.*

"Enterprise Zone", Earlstrees Industrial Development in 1984

## SCENE 2: BROKEN DREAMS

*This scene is a physical theatre depiction of Factory Work, set to the song "Broken Dreams", with moving images taken from a promotional 1980s CBC video entitled "Corby Works", intercut with Anglia News footage.*

*It is 1984. Five of the now-redundant Canteen Workers from Act One, ANNIE, KAREN, JEAN, YVONNE and ISOBEL, are Working with other women, JAN and JOSIE, in a Box Factory in Corby's new Enterprise Zone.*

*The music starts. During the song, the women enter the Factory dispiritedly, take off their coats, put on Work Hats and take their place at the Conveyor Belt. They mime the repetitive, boring, tiring Work of Assembling boxes.*

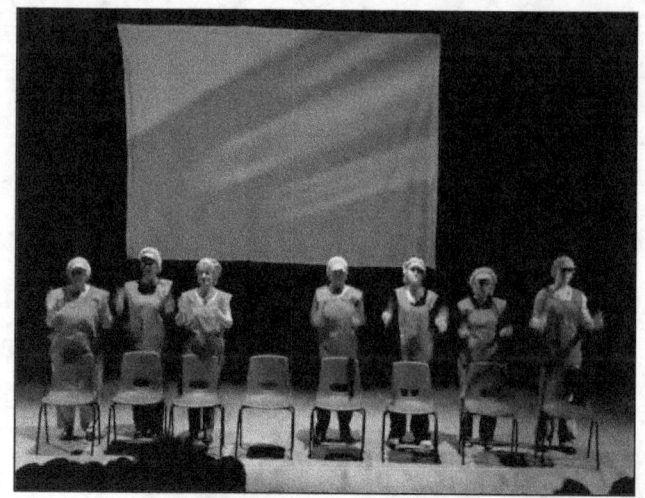

Big fish...

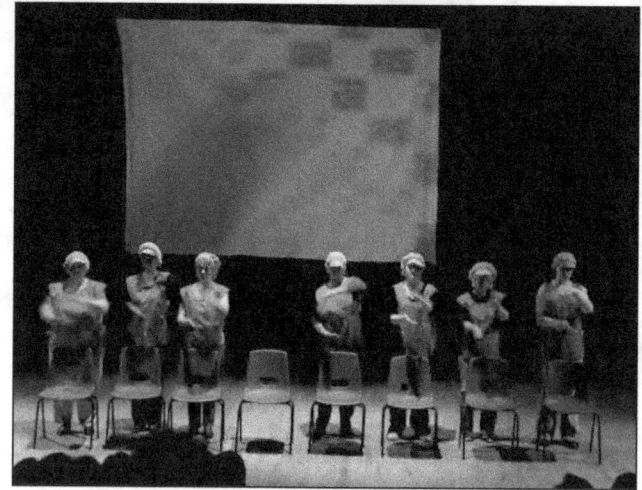

...little fish...

...cardboard box!

SONG: BROKEN DREAMS[18]
(Recording, from Banner Theatre's 1994 play "Sweatshop",
with voice montage between verses and at the end)

*It's women's Work and we come real cheap*
*Part-time, part-paid, bottom of the heap*
*Pin money? Well, that's a joke*
*Slogging your guts out for one more bloke*
*Working all day for the capitalist*
*And then back home to do another shift*
*No-one noticed the Work we did*
*Packing and Cleaning and Raising the kids*
*The last to be hired and the first to be sacked*
*disposable workers off the rack*
*And the men kept the men's Jobs just for the men*
*While we get the scrag ends all over again*

VOICE OF WORKER (*on recording*): Every day it's depressing, you see Job losses every day on the television, we've been wiped out...

*We worked on your Looms and your Rolling Mills*
*Toiled in your Shipyards to pay our bills*
*In your Deep Seam Mines we sweated blood*
*Night Shift, Day Shift - you screwed us good*
*Picked your fruit and Ploughed your land*
*Built Power Stations and Hydro Dams*
*Schools, Hospitals, Motorways*
*We sold our life's blood to earn our pay*
*Now you're pulling out, the future's gone*
*To Seoul, Jakarta, Beijing, Taiwan*
*God save the queen and the union jack*
*Like the Factory Gates we're up for scrap.*

VOICE OF WORKER (*on recording*): You have to have 4 "O" levels now to be a Dustbin Man...

*We Laboured with craft, we Laboured with Skill*
*Now we queue at the Job Club with time to kill*
*Jobs on Security now and again*
*Chicken Pluckers or Lollipop Men*
*You can train to Wash Dishes, you can train to Clean*
*Or be a brain surgeon on some bloody scheme*
*When the training's done it's "sorry chuck*
*No Jobs here, shove off, tough luck!"*

*Ten quid a day, no holiday pay*
*No cards, no Union, no bloody way!*
*We've sold our lives to the big machine*
*And we're left with nothing but broken dreams*
*Broken dreams, broken dreams...*

*The women turn to the screen.*

VOICES OF WORKERS *(on recording)*: £3.60 an hour... paid buttons for money... £2.75 per hour... buttons for money... £2.05... £2.05... that is disgusting... £1.74 an hour... below Union rates... 40p a skirt... Union rates... 10p for putting a zip on... disgusting... 2600 rupiahs a day... treated like dirt... one dollar a quarter... treated like dirt... 6p an hour... minimum wages... 0.3 pence per solder joint - that is disgusting... disgusting!

CORBY COUNCILLOR TOM MACKINTOSH *(on film):* I think you'll find... a lot of people in the town... especially unemployed people are looking for - not cheap Jobs... not Jobs with low pay... they're looking for a future...

*The women get their coats, and then rearrange chairs for the next scene to suggest a room where they have come for their break. They chat naturally and eventually sit down.*

## SCENE 3: THE AFTERMATH

*This scene is an unbroken continuation of Scene 2, with everyone remaining in place.*

JEAN: We haven't got long.

JAN: I've had a reply from the Miners' Wives Support Group in Castleford, West Yorkshire... to say we can come up next weekend.

JEAN: Read it then.

JAN *(reads letter):*
"Dear Sisters,
You would be very welcome to come and talk to us about how you have survived since the Closure of The Steelworks. We are having a do next Saturday, as it looks like both Glass Oughton and Lekston Luck Pits are on the hit list for Closure. Thanks for your support and your kind donations. We are taking the kids to Scarborough on a trip with the money.
In solidarity,
Susan Perry
Secretary, Castleford Miners' Wives Support Group."

So we better practise what we want to say![19]

JEAN: Go on then, you first.

*Women take it in turns to get up as if on stage and practise what they will say to the Miners' Wives.*

KAREN: Four years on and where have we got to? Men at home watching TV or down the pub. Being expected to adapt to making the dinner instead of making Steel.

Self-esteem gone. Their role as breadwinner... provider... man - changed forever.

Men lost their identity

Whilst we women work all the hours that God sends for some cowboy firm who'll just up sticks and move when their subsidy has run out.

Jobs for women a-plenty. The boss gets away with part-time hours and pays us less – any hint of Union organisation and you're out the door. And none of us will fight it cos we're too desperate to hold down the Job.

Women Workers in a Chocolate Factory in the 1940s

The Workers' Rights Group[20] is leafleting outside the Factories trying to get a foothold. But the Unions have been silenced since The Works closed.

Left out of the discussions about bringing Jobs to the town. We don't want Jobs at any price! We want secure Jobs – new Jobs, not ones just moved here from elsewhere.

The Union was a way of life down The Works. There was a whole support network... and benefits... and community – a safety net. Now it is everyone for themselves. I'm all right, Jack! Divide and rule.[21]

Unionised women Workers Striking in the 1920s

115

JEAN: Of course - Maggie's started on the Miners now.[22] Her... and that butcher Ian McGregor. It'll be the Dockers next! We know what it's like to have the guts ripped out of your community.

The least we can do is give our support. You were there for us when we needed you. Return the favour! Stand together! I'm out collecting food for the Striking Miners most nights. And we women have started a committee to bring Miners' kids here for a holiday.

Tucking in at a Soup Kitchen

Dissuading a vehicle from crossing the Picket Line during the 1980 Steel Strike in Corby

I remember the Steel Strike as if it was yesterday. And I bet there's the same family battles going on as we had. There's brothers who still don't speak even now. It's the principle! I can't believe people don't understand the need for Solidarity... but I suppose everyone had their own valid reasons for doing what they did. It was hard to manage without any money... despite the food parcels and bags of veg from the wholesalers.

I remember my Frank took a parcel round to one Striker. Older lady... on her own... no family support. And the following week we heard she'd killed herself. Pulled the electric fire in the bath with her.

It's the selfish bastards I don't understand... the ones who never even tried. The boss's darling!
I hope the Miners realise that Redundancy Pay – no matter how many noughts they put on the end of it – runs out eventually... and you're left with nothing – no Industry and no future.

Women Against Pit Closures

ANNIE: It's the kids I worry for. By the time they leave school the whole idea of a proper Job, a Job for life – Comrades, Workmates, common Trades and Skills to bind you together – will have gone. Call that progress? It's gone backwards – not forwards.

Comrades in the Workplace

Back to the days of the Dockers[23] standing in pens on the Docks waiting to be picked for a day's Labour.

Dockers' Picket, 1930s

These new agencies are a rip-off! They get a huge profit for every Worker they send on a thirteen-week trial. No ties for the employer. No sick pay, holiday pay, maternity pay – no security! My pal went for an interview at one place that had 3,000 applicants for seventy Jobs! They expect you to be available for Work at the drop of a hat.

Employment Agencies

There's plenty of Work on these new Twilight Shifts. Mind you – that's when the kids are in and home from school. And unless your man is on the dole and will watch them while you go out to Work it's back to latchkey kids… The pair of you out Working, and the kids left to their own devices. Bringing themselves up, they were. No wonder there's all this "drugs and teenage mums."

JOSIE: My man went for retraining – he's nearly done as an Accountant.

Sometimes I have to pinch myself. What a journey!

From Blast-furnaceman using his bulk, body and brawn – he's a big man, is my Ernie – to an Accountant! I'm surprised that he still has a brain left to do it with after the amount of drinking he did with all that Redundancy Pay. Nearly split us up, it did.

A Steelworker

Well, I'd just finished a degree myself.[24] I was sick of being thought of as thick – so I went back to school. I graduated the day the Closure was announced! Brought up my three children and then decided it was my turn. I thought I'd be able to find a decent Job that paid more than the pin money we get here. We don't even get equal pay. And you can forget Graduate Employment. They see Corby folk as "factory fodder". So much for getting an education to better yourself. I'm worried he'll not get a Job at the end of his course either.

A mature student graduate, mother of 3

I mean... surely Accounting is a middle-class profession. How the hell will he find the experience – the contacts! I hoped this would give him a better control of the family purse – but no – it still falls to me to balance it up.

The lure of the horses

ELAINE: At least she's got something to balance up. My Johnny got £20,000 Redundancy Money[25]. He invested it – in the bloody bookie's! Lost the lot. So it's me out earning the Wages now, and the lazy bugger won't lift a finger to help in the house. The gambling's nothing new. He's always done it. We've never had a penny. Folk used to look down on us. But we're every bit as good as they are.

I remember when we women would get a bus on a Friday at 12 o'clock – specially laid on, down to the Wages Office - to stand and wait with your hands open, to make sure your man coughed up the Wages before he got down the pub or the bookie's.

Special bus for women to go and get the wages

Some of them used to be too ashamed to go home after going on a bender and spendin' it all – so they'd go back and sleep on the Shop Floor, tell the wife they were doing overtime. The other men would bring in food and sure enough... they'd Work like a Navvy to make up some pay. Many a couple came to blows about the Wages being pissed up against the wall. Saturday night up the Labour Club. *(She remembers.)*

It wasn't unheard of for people to go off with someone else... ships that pass in the night. It was lonely at home, so you sought comfort where you could get it.

Night Shifts meant absence from the marital bed

Silly buggers wouldn't be able to keep their mouths shut though, and they would go into Work bragging about it. But that's men for you!

YVONNE: OK, let's talk about the money – how do you go from tipping up what's left of your wages to handling thousands? The banks have moved in here like sharks – off-shore banks, and Irish banks. Some men did invest wisely.

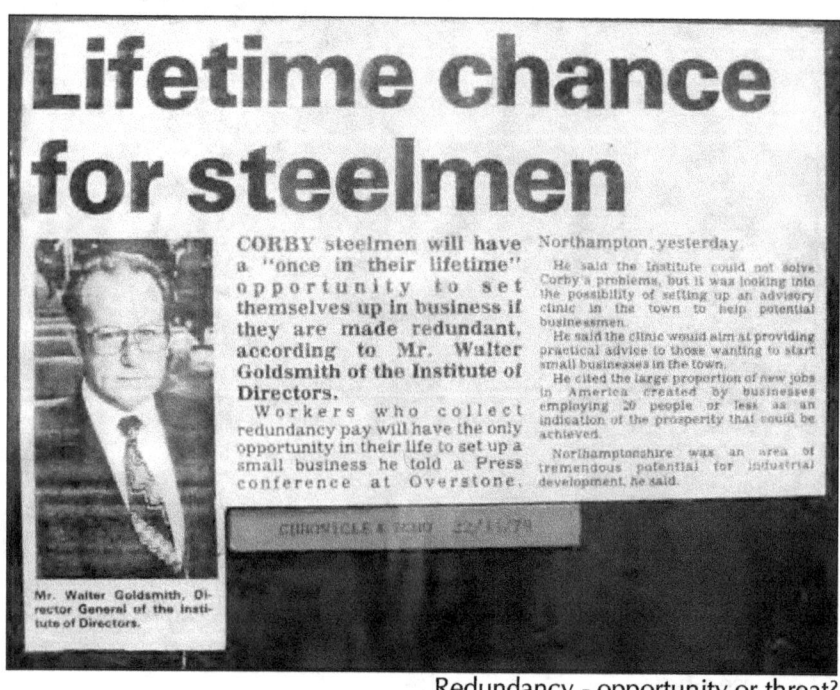

Redundancy - opportunity or threat?

Like my Robert. We bought our house and I had my last child knowing it had a roof over its head. Some of my neighbours just disappeared - couldn't keep up the payments. Moonlighting, they called it. Put the keys to the house through the estate agent's door and headed off to a new life somewhere else.

I reckon The Works closing was a godsend to some men. They had a chance to set up as self-employed. Be their own boss. A good few went out on the taxis. And they'll all be in Work once they start on that WonderWorld. It'll be great for the kids.

The place looks different too with all these clean, shiny new Factories.

I do miss the Corby Candle, though. My youngest used to watch that at night before she went to sleep.

The Corby Candle

But I don't miss the dirt. My washing's a lot cleaner now, I can tell you!

ISOBEL: My man's make-up pay ran out last year. He still has no chance of a decent Job here. So he's off to Holland, where his mate tells him Jobs are ten a penny. Imagine, British Workers ending up as immigrant Labour![26]

Commonwealth immigrants, 1948

Mind you - the pay's better... and the conditions! And at the end of the day, we were all immigrants here in Corby.

My daughter's just come back from her travels and the first thing she noticed was the number of new X-reg gold Ford Granadas… And the houses – extensions, porches, conservatories, own front door! The town is changing, that's for sure. Affluence on the one hand… whilst other areas are virtually derelict.

Home improvements, paid for with redundancy money

Mind you... you can buy flats and houses in those areas for next to nothing. Some people have bought two or three and converted them to amazing living spaces.

Before

...and after

And not just those with redundancy money to spare! People are still coming to Corby for a chance of a better life. One man up the Lincoln came down from Glasgow looking for Work. Seven thousand men on the dole! But he was lucky. He got a Job - on the buses. Lived in a caravan and as soon as he had money put by, he bought two properties on Blenheim Walk - a real no-go area – and did them up. His own sprawling urban palace.

The family joined him as soon as it was ready. To him it was paradise.

He told me he was from "Muggers' Alley" in Glasgow.

"Muggers' Alley", Corby style

So however much we think the town is going downhill, it is as full of opportunity as ever.

## SCENE 4: STAND YOUR GROUND

*The following scene is based upon the true story of the formation of the Corby Clothing Company in 1984.*

*The women rearrange the chairs to suggest a bank of Industrial Sewing Machines at the Lodiva Factory on Earlstrees Industrial Estate. Now playing different workers - SUSAN, MARGARET, BETTY, LIZZIE, JOY, IRENE and EVELYN - they mime working in a dismal Sewing Factory whilst a SUPERVISOR monitors them closely.*

*The song "Sweatshop" plays on the soundtrack while images of global Sweatshops are projected on the screen behind the women.*

SONG: SWEATSHOP
(Recording, from Banner Theatre's 1994 play "Sweatshop")

*Working in a Sweatshop, bottom-line Wages*
*Down on the Factory Floor*
*Working in a Sweatshop, non-stop rip-off*
*Ain't gonna take no more!*

*Acid and grime, double overtime*
*Stinking fumes all the day*
*Hands in a rash trying to earn my cash*
*Burning my life away*
*Just do the Job, don't open your gob*
*Plenty more where you came from*
*The more you sweat, the less you get*
*Smethwick, Dundee, Taiwan*

*Working in a Sweatshop, bottom-line Wages*
*Down on the Factory Floor*
*Working in a Sweatshop, non-stop rip-off*
*Ain't gonna take no more!*

*Two pounds an hour, working for this shower*
*Stuck like a dog in a ditch*
*Non-stop grind, killing my mind*
*To keep this boss-man rich*
*Don't want a Union - says it's gonna ruin him*
*He ain't gonna pay a penny more*
*He's in clover, in his big Rover*
*That's how the poor stay poor*

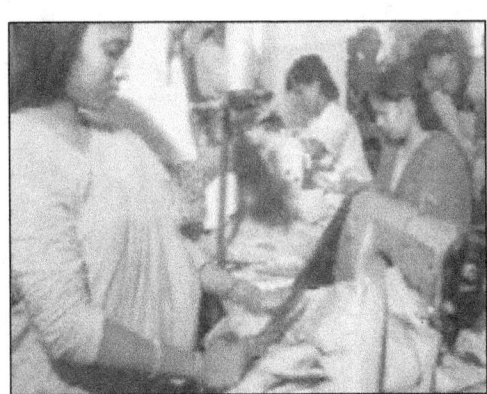 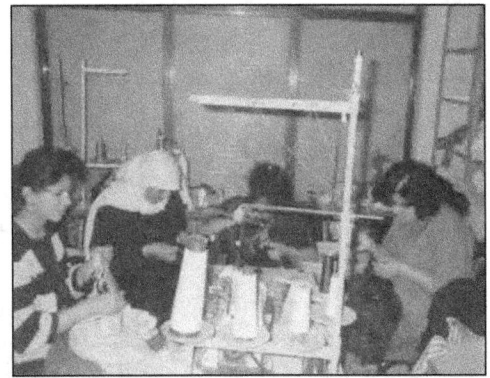

*Working in a Sweatshop, bottom-line Wages*
*Down on the Factory Floor*
*Working in a Sweatshop, non-stop rip-off*
*Ain't gonna take no more!*

*Instrumental break*

*Hey there Jimmy man, what you gonna gimme man?*
*You ain't gonna get your way*
*No more enslavement, we're out on the pavement*
*And we are here to stay!*

*Aggravation, intimidation*
*Down on the Picket Line*
*Scabs won't break us, cops won't shake us*
*Come sun, rain or shine!*

● Determined to succeed - (from left) Veronica MacLeod, Maureen McQuillan, Susan McCready and Ellen McAvoy.

*Fed up with the SUPERVISOR's nit-picking, the women take an unscheduled break. They re-gather outside the Factory as the music fades out, and ad lib their complaints about the SUPERVISOR.*

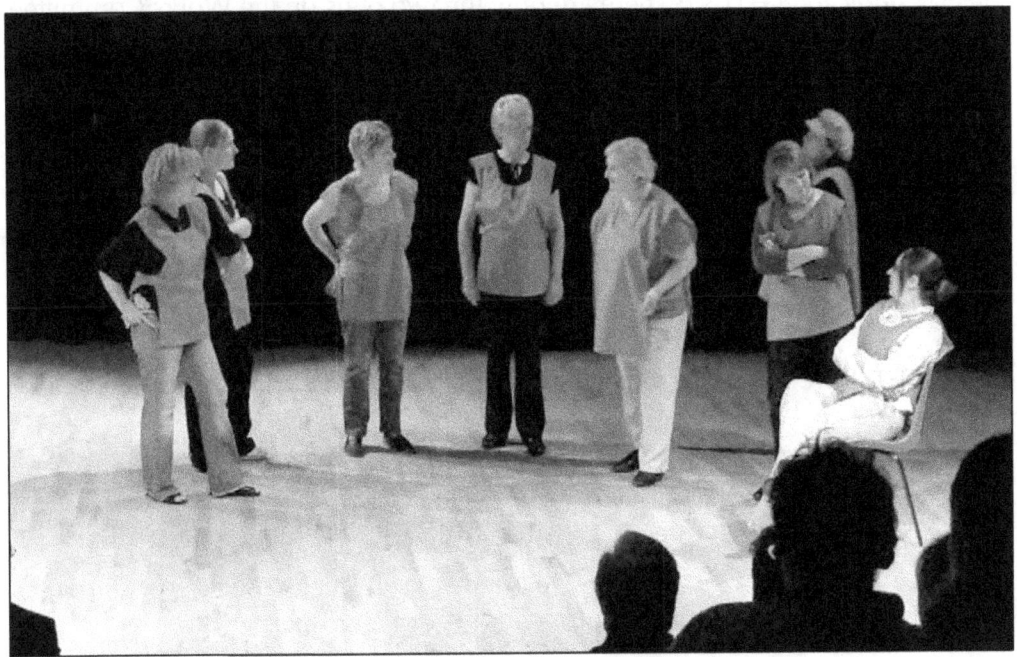

*Enter ELLEN, the Union Rep.*

ELLEN: Ladies, can I have your attention? I've just had a meeting with the managing director and he says there is not enough money to pay your Wages this week - and the state this company is in, I think we're heading for another Redundancy.

SUSAN: I've been made redundant three times in five years. I've had enough!

MARGARET: What are we meant to live off?

BETTY *(entering from the Factory)*: There's something fishy going on. I've just seen some of the lads carrying some big bits of Machinery to a van out the back.

ELLEN: What did I tell you!

JEAN: What are we going to do about it?

LIZZIE: We could run it better ourselves.

JOY: That's a bloody good idea. Why don't we?

IRENE: We could have a Sit-in.

ELLEN: If we took over the Factory they couldn't take the Machinery or make us Redundant.

EVELYN *(indicating* ELLEN*)*: There are only the two of us on the Works Committee. We'll need more than that to organise a Sit-in.

LIZZIE *(to* EVELYN*)*: I'll join you. I'll sort out food and a cleaning rota.

EVELYN: Anyone else?

BETTY: Yes, I'll sort out getting the kids collected from school.

ELLEN *(to* EVELYN*)*: Are you taking notes?

MARGARET: If we're staying the night I'll get my Robert to bring us in a tele and a radio.

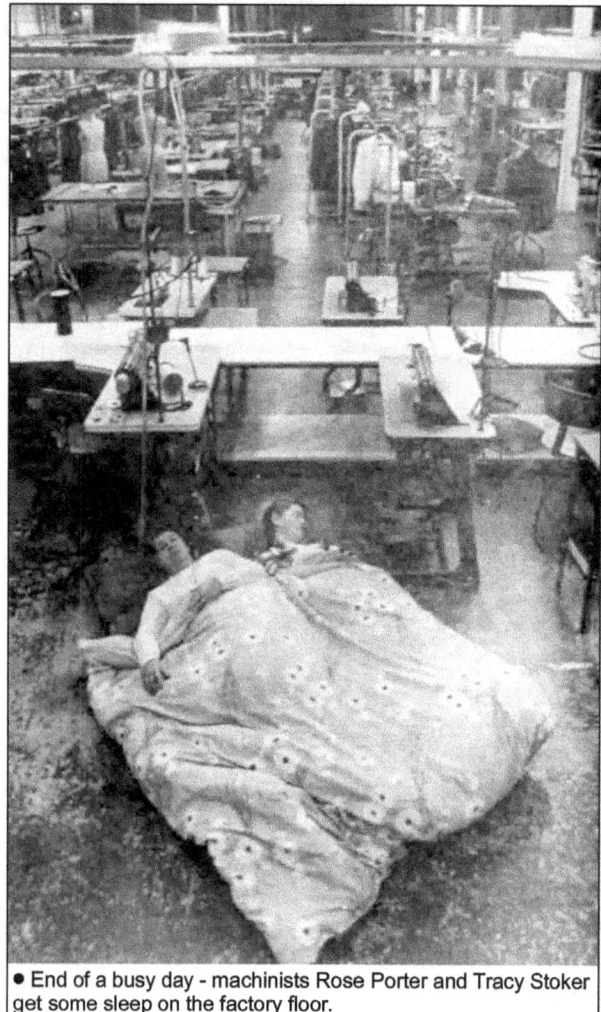

● End of a busy day - machinists Rose Porter and Tracy Stoker get some sleep on the factory floor.

IRENE: I'll get Eric to sort us some beds. He runs the Scouts. And I'll get someone to go round and get all our bedding and personal things.

ELLEN: I'll contact the Union. We'll need their support.

BETTY: I'm off to stop those lads taking the stuff. They need to be with us, guarding the Machinery - not getting rid of it.

IRENE *(to BETTY)*: I'll come with you.

JOY: Right, let's go.

ELLEN: Wait a minute! Legally, we can't do this. The managing director is still on the premises.

JOY *(sarcastically)*: Well, let's invite Mr Azimi to take a break. He never bothered striking up a working relationship with us. He forgets we're human beings. Anyone fancy coming with me to kick him out?

ELLEN: I'll come with you.

*They all re-enter the Factory and line up facing the audience with arms crossed.*

*A film clip (excerpt from Anglia News report, September 1984) is shown on the screen.*

NEWS REPORTER *(on film)*: When last week's Wages weren't paid, Workers say it became clear that the project would fold and they would be left without Jobs or Redundancy Money.

A sign outside the Factory states: "THIS FACTORY IS CONTROLLED BY THE NATIONAL UNION OF TAILORS AND GARMENT WORKERS".[27]

Today it's business pretty much as usual, with Office Staff doing the paperwork, and all the sixty-two strong Workforce staying on. Workers are confident that orders will continue to pay their Wages, but they are hoping for a buyer to take them on, the Machinery - and their customers. The Union is confident that the company is viable and they say they have had several enquiries about it.

COLIN TINDLEY *(Union Official of the NUT and GW, on film)*: Well, within the last hour we have been visited by a prospective employer. I've told him the worst that he could know because I don't want anybody to be caught by surprise - and he is showing a very keen interest. We are arranging for the owners of the Machinery to rush here now, so we can arrange a meeting with them.

NEWS REPORTER *(on film)*: The Workers are convinced that they can make a go of things. They say that all they need is the finance and good management to secure their future.

A UNION REP *(on film)*: Everybody concerned with the Factory, and even the past owners, are pleased that we did it. The Machinery is safe. Nothing is going to leave here without us knowing.

*End of film clip.*

## SONG: WONDERWORLD (Reprise)

*Here we are, it's a new decade*
*Guess what is the news?*
*The Council's issued an ultimatum*
*For what have they to lose?*
*We want to see some Building done*
*For we must now save face*
*But will the contractors ever listen to them?*
*Everyone watch this space*

*Welcome to WonderWorld*
*Welcome to WonderWorld*
*Welcome to WonderWorld*
*Welcome to WonderWorld*

*May the first has come and gone*
*No Builders have moved in*
*The Council's pulled the plug on them*
*Now British Steel are set to win*
*For the land they sold ten years ago*
*They can buy back for a song*
*Now with a profit of a hundred million pounds*
*You can hear the board sing along*

*Goodbye to WonderWorld*
*Goodbye to WonderWorld*
*Goodbye to WonderWorld*
*Goodbye to WonderWorld*

*All exit.*

# THE WASTED YEARS

### SCENE 5: A CHOCOLATE FACTORY IN CORBY, 1998
*by Emma Boulton Roe*

*Enter EMMA and JO, two women in their early 20s, meeting outside the chocolate factory on their break. JO is about to light a cigarette.*

EMMA: What you doing out here? Thought you quit?

JO: I did. I mean… I'm going to…

EMMA: Yeah, right!

JO: It's no use. I can't make it through these twilight shifts without one!

EMMA: I know. Me too. Can't afford it when I'm back at uni though…

JO: I actually look forward to the break from home, even if it is at a bloody factory!

EMMA: So how is the little one?

JO: He's fine. Teething, bless him. Which is mum-speak for crying all the time!

*Both laugh. Enter JEN, another young woman.*[28]

JO: Bloody hell! Look what the cat dragged in!

EMMA: Hi Jen! Haven't seen you for ages!

JEN: Hello girls! The Jenmeister is back in town!

EMMA and JO: Again!

*All laugh.*

EMMA: You run outta money then?

JEN: Yup. What? You think I'd be in this shit-hole if I was flush?

JO: Watch it! Some of us are here full-time!

EMMA: Speak for yourself! Holidays are enough for me. I can't wait to get back to uni…

JO: So where've you been this time? It wasn't somewhere hot, that's for sure! You've got a Corby tan. *(She laughs.)*

JEN: I've been to Iceland.

JO: My mum goes there every Saturday. They do great meal deals.

JEN *and* EMMA *groan*.

EMMA: How's your mum, Jen?

JO *nudges* EMMA. JEN *looks uncomfortable and turns to the audience.* JO *and* EMMA *freeze-frame during* JEN's *speech.*

JEN *(to audience):* I remember the first time I went away. It was to a refuge[29] in Wellingborough. Not quite the trip of a lifetime. Of course you always have to come back from these places. It must have stuck with me from an early age. If things get too much you can just get up and go - to a refuge, to another town, and things will be great for a while. Until HE found us - and then it was back to "normal life". Back to the reality of a violent, alcoholic dad and a scared mum who couldn't cope.

But if you go that little bit further… people can't find you. You can be free and do the things you never could.

And you can change your whole character. Nobody knows your past. You don't have to tell them anything. I can be happy Jen, always travelling cos she wants to see the world and experience everything.

Instead of THAT Jen with THAT dad. Jen who was found in the streets in her nightie, looking for her mum. Jen who is looking for answers to the questions that can't be answered.

I'd still rather be travelling than be here though. I come back when I run out of money. Spend time with my mum. I feel a bit guilty for leaving her. Go straight to the agencies, work all the shifts I can.

There's no loyalty on their part or mine. It's great. I get to work the system. Then, when I get enough money, I get out my map, close my eyes and let fate decide where I'm off to next.

Dad bought me that map when I was little. Half the places on it don't even exist any more!

That was when things were OK. When we were a normal family and he had a Job and we did normal things! It's scary how you can love someone as much as you hate them. That's why I keep the map. He'd wanted to travel. Was just about to leave when The Works closed - so he never got the chance. Grandad needed his support. It was hard for his family to adjust to life on the dole. And I kinda pity him…

He ruined his life - and my mum's. But in a messed-up way it forced me to do something with mine. I have experienced so much. This town keeps people here. I wouldn't be the person I am if I'd stayed here. But I wouldn't be the person I am without it either.

I'll do whatever it takes to keep me travelling[30], till I find somewhere I want to stay. And if that means packing chocolates for a few months… *(shrugs.)* At least I can leave when I want to…

*(To* JO *and* EMMA*):* So are you still allowed to eat as many of these as you want?

JO: Give it a few days, love, and you won't want any for the rest of your life!

EMMA *and* JEN *freeze-frame during the following speech.*

JO *(to audience):* What they don't realise is that I eat them at home as well. Why? Boredom. It's no fun bringing up kids on your own, you know! I'm really jealous that she's been travelling again. It's been years since I had a holiday and even then it was only to Calais with the school. I had my first hangover on that trip - I still can't drink whisky!

I got pregnant not long after we got back[31]. And when the baby arrived it pretty much put an end to any desire I had to go travelling.

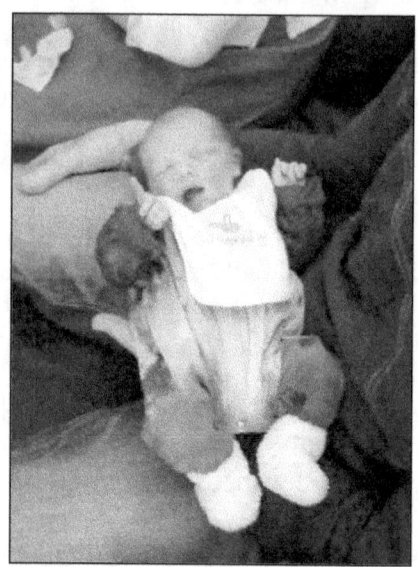

A night out is still a luxury! Literally every penny I have earned since I turned sixteen has gone on the girls. I don't blame them though. It's not their fault their dad doesn't give us any money. Don't get me wrong - my family have really helped over the years. They supported us financially as well as being there for babysitting and cheering me up.

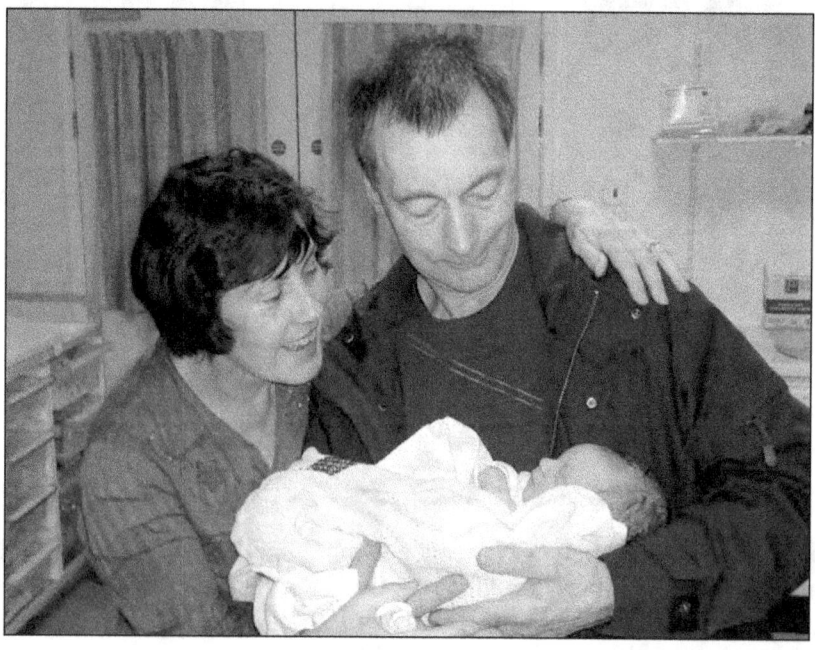

I don't understand how single mothers manage without a family to help them. But most people in Corby have a big family - or a community at least. That's the best thing about this town, community. Everyone from Corby is an outsider. They all came here for the works and no-one belonged here so they built up these little groups. Then the works shut and they came together as a town to fight and now Corby is more about the people than the place. Which is a good job, cos there's not much here to do.

It's no wonder we're all having babies so young - you have to find your own fun in Corby! It's a different story once the boys realise how much hard work having a family is though - they're all talk until responsibility kicks in. Craig didn't leave us straight away but I think that had more to do with not wanting other people to think bad of him. Instead he just started doing everything wrong. He never held down a job and spent all of our money on drugs, fags and Special Brew. Not that there were many jobs to hold down in the years after the works shut down.

I don't know, the older I get the more I think that he really was too young to start a family. He just couldn't handle the stress of never making ends meet and we both knew that no matter how hard we tried, things were never going to be that great for the girls.

I'm still trying my best for them. We have a lot of fun exploring the pretty bits all around Corby, like the woods, East Carlton Park and the Boating Lake. My Jade loves feeding the ducks.

Hopefully we'll get a cinema again, and some more stuff to do! It's hard enough finding a babysitter and the money to be able to go out - but then to have to travel to the next town to do it! I don't really bother. I go to my local and have a few drinks and that'll do me. For now. Dad tries to give me money to go out but I'd rather it got spent on nappies. Anyway I feel bad taking his money. He earns less than me at the minute!

Besides, there comes a point when you need to do it all on your own. I don't want to be living off them - I want to prove that, even though I'm a young single mum, I can look after us by myself. And I do. And it's hard, but we'll get by.

I never thought I'd end up working in a chocolate factory. I had wanted to be a teacher, but you can't take a baby to university. Maybe when my Amy goes to school next year I can think about it, do it part-time. That's if I can afford the fees!

They don't make it easy to better yourself, do they? And I'd have to go somewhere else to do it - nearly four hours a day on the bus is a bit much, and I can't really move. So I'll probably end up just staying here with the kids.

I do wonder what life would be like without the girls - but they didn't ask to be born, and it's not their fault I've got such bad taste in men. I'm mostly happy with the way things are, here with my family, in Corby.

*(To JEN and EMMA):* We'd best be getting back. Some of us can't afford to lose our jobs.

JEN: I'd better nip to the loo!

EMMA: I'll be there in a minute!

*Exit JO and JEN.*

EMMA *(to audience):* There's no way I could do this full-time. It would do my head in. They say that goldfish only grow as big as the size of the tank they're in. Corby always felt to me like a very small goldfish bowl. I wasn't comfortable being stunted. I always knew that I needed to do more than just stay in Corby and work a crap job in a factory. And I definitely wasn't going to raise my children here!

I mean, what chance would they have in life, growing up in this tiny, stagnant pond?

Kingswood

Imagine what would have happened to us all if we had a big lake full of life. How big we'd have all grown then!

I suppose it wasn't that bad at first. I wasn't really aware that Corby was different to any other town until I was old enough to go out with my friends. The shops used to be OK. We went to the swimming baths every week and would chat in the café afterwards.

All that exercise, followed by chips and four bars of chocolate! We had a cinema then too. I went on a date when I was fourteen to see *The Lion King!* I cried during that and had to pretend I had something in my eye... Oh, and the Quasar Laser! That was great!

But it didn't last very long. The cinema went. The Quasar went. Shops shut down and were replaced by card shops! What's that all about? How many cards does one town need? We did end up spending hours in Clinton's reading all the jokes though. Well, you've got to keep yourself amused somehow!

It's funny, but looking back on those times it was a blessing in very heavy disguise that my stepfather was so strict. I was so scared that I would be caught out doing something wrong that I never sought my amusement in parks with bottles of cider or worse, drugs. It's no wonder so many kids went off the rails. Not many had the money to get to Kettering with its shops and the Odeon and Kettering Leisure Village, and besides it took too long to get there. What were the kids supposed to do with all that pent-up energy? Mix that with teenage hormones and curiosity and it's a recipe for disaster.

We started to get a reputation. Corby kids! Hard. Mean. Violent. Always looking for trouble. Always looking for something to do, more like! Or guidance!

It wasn't just bad kids that got into trouble. I knew so many kids from good homes that ended up getting arrested. Gang warfare all over the town, fighting about turf. And no one tried to stop the fighting after what happened to Louise Allen.[32] We had police escorts after school when that happened! "You got one of ours, now we're gonna get one of you." You'd think it would have made people stop and think, but it only got worse. Someone always has to pay in this town. It's a never-ending cycle of blame and violence.

I began to hate everything about living here. The town had a really oppressive feel about it. I mean, we feature at the top of all the statistics[33] - teenage pregnancy, illiteracy, depression, alcoholism and mental health problems. Some legacy!

Aspiration was not a word recognised by my peers. I was lucky. I came from a family who believed in the value of education and would regularly tell me that any dream was within my reach. "They can't take what's inside your head," my grandad used to say. Conflicting messages came from my stepdad, who suffered with depression. He thought I should aim a little lower and that I had too much imagination. He tried to bring me back down to earth. Where apparently our careers advisor lived! I was discouraged from trying to follow any kind of creative route. Office work was OK. Aside from my complete lack of computer skills, you mean?

But grandad was right. You can't take knowledge and dreams and ambition away. Not if you believe in them. And I did. I still do. I worked hard at school. I knew my only route out of Corby was via university.[34]

And then they scrapped the grants system the year before I went. I knew so many people who wanted to go but couldn't afford it. Means testing worked for me. I don't have to pay fees but it meant I had to get a student loan.

Debt. What a great start in life! But I'm out there. Living my dream. A little fish in a big pond. And I love it!

*She exits.*

## THE PRESENT DAY

### SCENE 6: STEEL KIDS

*Enter* YOUNG NARRATOR *and twelve other young people, all wearing black t-shirts with a bold white "Steel Kids" logo. They depict, through physical theatre, the following poem set to projected images.*

YOUNG NARRATOR:
>There's a Spirit in this town
>Which comes from the Steel.
>A recipe for resistance.

From the Ore
Dug from the bowels of the Earth,
Molten, burned and beaten into shape,
A smooth, shiny, indestructible Tube emerges.

We take the knocks, the blows, the hammering.
The Fire rages within.
Stops us fitting, accepting the crumbs.

Some give the knocks, the blows, the hammerings.
They become famous:
CORBY KEEP OUT![35]
Not for the faint-hearted!

The Works is gone.
No-one bothers to tend the Steel now.
The Tubes is always under threat:
But the Ore remains,
And the Fire!
Give us the right treatment and we will endure
and emerge as the best and most resilient there is.

Leave us as the raw stuff
And the alchemy will never tame the rage.
Add to that our Celtic roots -
Race memory of domination...

... and maybe you'll understand

THE STEEL KIDS!

# The Future

SCENE 7: THE FUTURE

*Enter* DEVELOPER, *a middle-aged white man in a suit. The* STEEL KIDS *cluster round him as he addresses them.*

DEVELOPER:    Why so glum? I'm your chum!
              Come with me, you will see
              Demolition on the go
              Corby Town will be on show

Big-name stores you know and love... card shops all will get the shove

A swimming pool, Olympic style... a cinema to make you smile

New roads and rail link, buses too... real transport here for me and you

New schools by top designers made... for these, already plans are laid

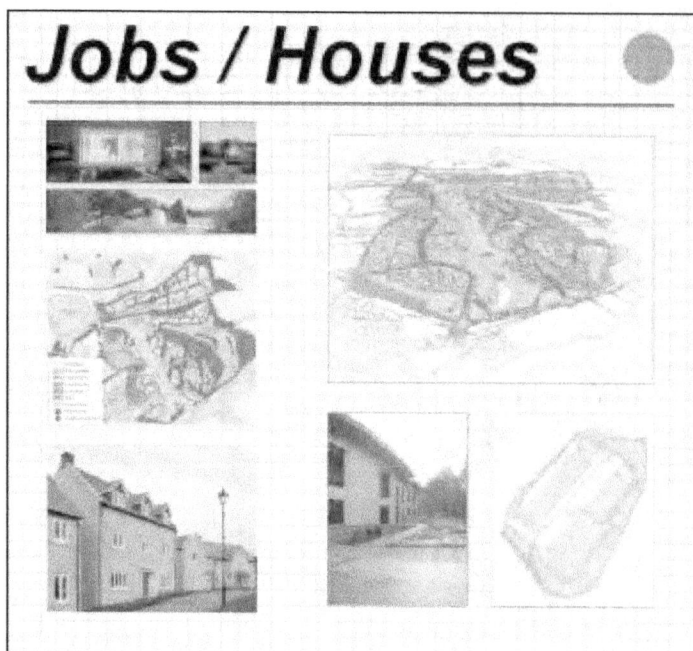

Good Jobs and houses eco-style... to build all this will take a while

So tell me please just what you think... I'll write it down in pen and ink!

## Consultation

**We want to know what YOU have to say**

**We welcome your questions and comments...**

STEEL KIDS *(to* DEVELOPER*)*: Here's our reality clearly on show - what exactly was it you wanted to know?

An empty town centre with nowhere to shop...

Some DIY leisure, there isn't a lot!

163

A taxi, the rail link,
a bus now and then…

And schools which
keep changing…
the question is, when?[36]

And some of our houses are being knocked down... so rich and posh people can move to our town.

You ask for our views,
So yes, we'll play our part
All we ask is - please listen,
They come from the heart!

*The* STEEL KIDS *lead the* DEVELOPER *to a seat and all watch as various* STEEL KIDS *present their views in the following three scenes.*

## SCENE 8: I WISH
*by Kirsty Graham, aged 12*

*Enter* KIRSTY.

KIRSTY:
I tried to think whether people in other places have more than I have here in Corby.
But I realised I didn't know anyone in a different place in the world.
I went to school in Uppingham for a bit.
But all the people I knew there were from Corby.
So I only know Corby people.
I don't mind.

I know we don't have a bowling alley,
a cinema,
and buses after 6.30.
But Corby is a great place.
And I don't care about those things -
as long as I have my friends and family
I'll be OK!

If I lived in London I'd have pollution and crime,
but here in Corby we have the woods,
the boating lake
and loads and loads of youth clubs to keep us out of trouble.

Mind you,
if I did live in a different place in the world,
I would have
a bowling alley,
a cinema,
and buses after 6.30.
And I would have people coming to see my town
instead of me having to go here and there
just for leisure facilities.

When I think about it,
my parents used to have
a bowling alley,
a cinema,
and buses after 6.30.
So why haven't we got them now?[37]
What happened?

I do have a wish to go to a different place in the world.
And I suppose it would be nice to have
a bowling alley,
a cinema,
and buses after 6.30 …
Hmmm… I wish!

*She exits.*

A bowling alley,

a cinema,

and buses after 6.30

## SCENE 9: 'TIL THE END
### by Jack Boulton Roe

*Enter* PHIL *and* JEN. *They sit back-to-back and speak as if on the phone to each other:* JEN *has just moved to Newcastle and is phoning her old friend* PHIL *back home in Corby.*[38] *Behind them stand two young actors who represent their* INNER VOICES.

PHIL: Hello?

JEN: Hi Phil, it's me. Guess what?

PHIL: Who?

JEN: It's Jen! Anyway -

PHIL (*cutting her off*): Oh! Jen! Hi. Haven't heard from you for ages. Thought you'd forgotten me! How's life in the city?

JEN: That's what I'm trying to tell you. It's great here. I've been soooo busy!

PHIL: Yeah, me too. On Thursday I -

JEN (*cutting him off*): On Thursday I went shopping in the city centre. I found this great pair of shoes in Primark - but they didn't have my size. Imagine that? I mean size 5 isn't exactly uncommon. And they were only twenty pounds. Anyway it don't matter cos I went to this great party at Cassie's. I don't really like her, but she begged me, so I thought what the hell! Anyway -

PHIL: Hang on! Hang on! What the hell is Primark?

JEN: Oh yeah, you don't have one in Corby… Well it's a cool shop. So yesterday I went swimming with Cat and Mark -

PHIL: Swimming! Yeah I went -

JEN: Mark is well fit, I tell you. Then I went bowling!

PHIL (*disappointed*): Oh. Bowling…

JEN: And today I saw that da Vinci thingy.

PHIL: Yeah, *The Da Vinci Code!* I saw that! Sure, it's good!

JEN: Well… I didn't really get it… but I suppose it's all right…

PHIL (*disappointed*): Oh…

JEN *and* PHIL *freeze-frame.*

JEN'S INNER VOICE:
>When I first escaped from Corby I couldn't hide the joy
>The sky was the limit and the world was my toy
>Now I've come back down to earth
>I realise it's just a different kind of trap.
>
>Though this is everything I used to long for
>Being here has left me overwhelmed and unfulfilled
>I thought this was freedom, I was wrong -
>I'll never be free.
>
>Though I wear a mask to fool the world
>In a second I'd exchange all this
>For one wasted moment on a forgotten street corner
>God, it sounds like bliss.
>But I'm stuck here 'til the end.

PHIL'S INNER VOICE:
        The future for the people of this town
        Is simple, pre-decided and set in stone.
        We are destined to long for better things
        Whilst refusing to realise we are trapped.

        There is a code in this town, a way of life
        Any attempt to improve it
        Is met with resistance, struggle and strife
        And I'll never be free.

        Though I long for crowded streets, flashing lights
        And good old entertainment
        I have resigned myself to boredom, envy and regret
        This is my home - I love it, despite the flaws
        And I'm stuck here 'til the end.

JEN *(to* PHIL, *on phone, sarcastically)*: So what's going on in your neck of the woods?

PHIL: Well, I went shopping…

JEN: Oooh! Where?

PHIL *(embarrassed):* Er… Home Bargains…

*All four exit.*

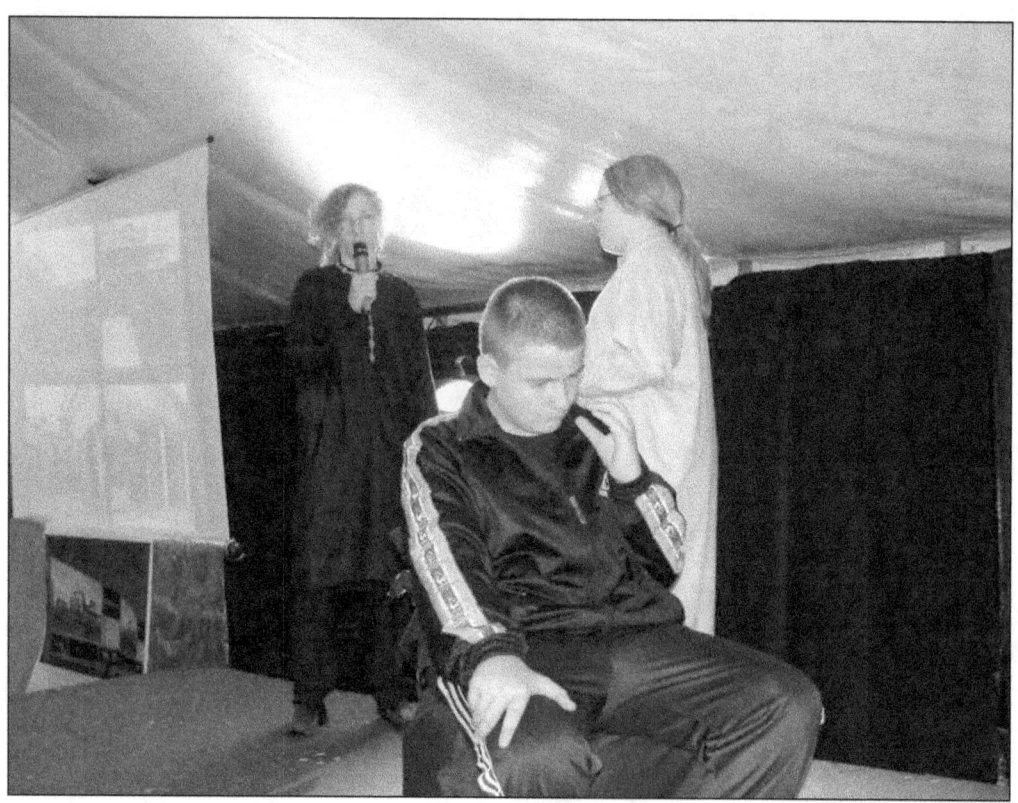

## SCENE 10: A CUT ABOVE

*This scene is an improvised comedy sketch.* LEE *and* JENNIFER, *two eighteen-year-olds, enter and sit down to discuss their future career options.*[39]

*They decide to try Hairdressing, which they think is an easy option and a route to fame and fortune.*

They then attempt to wash and cut a model's hair on their first day at Hairdressing college.

They end up accidentally dyeing her hair lurid colours and chopping it all off. They beat a hasty retreat.

*Enter* JODIE *and* JORIS, *two more sensible eighteen-year-olds. They tell their stories to the audience as two intercut monologues.*

JODIE: I feel sorry for them.
　　　That was me a year ago.
　　　I had dreams too.
　　　I wanted to be a Graphic Designer.

JORIS: I wanted to work in the Music Industry.

JODIE: Had to go to Kettering for that.

JORIS: Had to go to Northampton for that.

JODIE: Every day on the bus
　　　I kept being late
　　　And I couldn't afford my bus fares -
　　　Mum and Dad cut my pocket money at sixteen.

JORIS: Every day on the bus
　　　Up at the crack of dawn -
　　　Good practice for being on tour.
　　　I was lucky I got a bus pass.

JODIE:  So after a year I dropped out.
        My turn to find a Job - a good Job.
        Not just any Job.
        I had dreams!

        Oh yes!
        Plenty of low-paid agency jobs
        For twelve weeks at a time.
        But I wanted a future.
        If I couldn't be a Graphic Designer
        I wanted something that would teach me a Skill.

JORIS:  There were loads of Corby kids at the start of the year
        But most of them dropped out.
        I was determined to stick it.
        I knew the Music Industry was tough -
        Far harder than getting up early every day.

        I didn't mix with the students on other courses.
        Something about Musicians -
        We hung out together.
        And there was often band practice
        On top of the rest of the lessons and coursework.
        The Performing Arts lot were the same.
        People don't realise the extras involved
        In Music, Dance and Drama -
        Dedication.

JODIE:  Mum was a stay-at-home mum.
        Dad was on the buses -
        That always looked interesting.
        His mate told me they were looking for Apprentice Mechanics.
        I really fancied that idea -
        I'd always enjoyed tinkering about with cars.
        So I applied -
        And got it!

JORIS:  Worst of all was people trying to shatter my dreams.
        "You're seventeen and starry-eyed," one teacher said.
        That was like a red rag to a bull.
        Don't try and tell me what I can't do before I even try!
        "You'll never make it!" said my stepdad.
        "Get yourself a Trade and a proper Job."
        His story.
        He'd wanted to Act, but his dad made him get a Trade.

JODIE: Look at me now -
    The only girl down the depot.
    I love every minute of it
    And at the end of it
    I'll have a Trade that I can use anywhere in the world.
    Yes, I have dreams too.

JORIS: Through it all my mum stuck by me.
    She took on an extra shift to help pay my way
    And she's always singing and encouraging me with my music.
    She told me to follow my dreams, reach for the stars
    So I'm still there -
    Every day on the bus, practising my rhythms.
    Listening to my music, writing lyrics
    And I'll make my dream come true –
    Watch this space!

DEVELOPER: OK, we're listening and we'll take account.
    Work hard, take risks, and no amount
    Of effort will stand in our way
    To make for you a better day.
    We'll make it work, I promise that,
    And Maggie will not eat her hat!
    We believe in Corby Town
    And will not ever let you down.
    I still see doubt, that's cool and clear -
    Just watch this space this time next year!

*All exit.*

### SCENE 11: HOPE FOR THE FUTURE

*Enter the STEEL KIDS. They recite the following poem in unison.*

STEEL KIDS:   Look to the future[40]
Gleaming and bright
Though we've no Corby Candle
To light up the night

But a chance to improve it
A chance it can grow
Into somewhere we're proud of
Like you used to know.

When coming from Corby
Was no badge of shame
But a proud Town of Steel
To which everyone came

Who was looking for Work,
For a house, for a life
From all over the world
For a break from the strife
Of communities lacking
The things that we had.
Looking at it like that –
Who says Corby's bad?

We're your hope for the future
So please get it right -
Build a town we'll be proud of
Rekindle the light
That once welcomed all comers
To Old Corby Town.

*The* WOMEN *of the cast join the* STEEL KIDS *on stage.*

WOMEN: No WonderWorld this time -
Please don't let them down.
The Steel Kids of Corby
And all those who are new
Would do well to remember
What we've all lived through.

## SONG: GIVE US A JOB TO DO IN CORBY[41]

ALL *sing:*

> We've made this town our home
> Children and families
> Built it on hopes and dreams
> Built it on Iron Ore
> Now that we've come of age
> Give us what is our due
> Pay us a living Wage in Corby[42]
>
> Give us something now
> Some hope for a future
> So our children will have a chance
> In Corby

*All exit.*

*Curtain.*

# Author's Notes
Commentary, Additional Information and More Stories of Steel

# CONTENTS

## ACT ONE

### THE EARLY YEARS . . . . . . . . . 188

1. Labourers from Great Yarmouth . . . . . 188
2. Bevin Boys . . . . . . . . . 188
3. Industrial disease and the true cost of Steel . . . 190
4. Shift Work . . . . . . . . . 192
5. Glaswegian dialect . . . . . . . 193
6. Industrial accidents and Workers' Memorial Day . . 194
7. Women in the Steel Industry . . . . . . 198
8. Estate renewal, compulsory removal, or time to move on . 200
9. Works social . . . . . . . . 201
10. As The Works Grows . . . . . . . 201
11. Corby New Town in its heyday . . . . . 201

### SAVE OUR STEEL . . . . . . . . 202

12. Closure announced . . . . . . . 202
13. ROSAC . . . . . . . . . 205
14. The Strike . . . . . . . . . 208
15. Policing . . . . . . . . . 209
16. The Steel Strike in context: Trade Union history . . 213
17. Demolition . . . . . . . . 214

## ACT TWO

### STAND YOUR GROUND . . . . . . . 216

18. Banner Theatre . . . . . . . . 216
19. Working Class women speak out . . . . . 216
20. Workers' Rights Group . . . . . . . 217
21. Trade Unions today . . . . . . . 218
22. The 1984 Miners' Strike . . . . . . 219
23. Dockers' history . . . . . . . . 222
24. Which degree? . . . . . . . . 222
25. Redundancy settlement . . . . . . 222
26. Immigration . . . . . . . . 223
27. Sit-in at Corby Clothing Company . . . . . 223

LEGACY OF THE "WASTED YEARS" . . . . . . 224

28. Routes for young people . . . . . . 224
29. Domestic abuse . . . . . . . . 224
30. Travel tips . . . . . . . . . 226
31. Pregnancy testing and teenage parenting . . . . 228
32. Louise Allen . . . . . . . . 229
33. Statistics about Corby . . . . . . . 229
34. The education route . . . . . . . 231
35. Corby's reputation . . . . . . . 232

LOOK TO THE FUTURE . . . . . . . 234

36. New schools for Corby . . . . . . 234
37. Plans for new leisure facilities . . . . . 236
38. More shops for Corby . . . . . . . 238
39. Further education plans for Corby . . . . . 240
40. Corby's future and the forces of global capitalism . . 242
41. The Jobs market in Corby today . . . . . 245
42. Wages and conditions . . . . . . . 246


MISCELLANEOUS . . . . . . . . 248

Creative Process and Afterword . . . . . . 248
Cast Lists . . . . . . . . . 256
Comments from Cast Members . . . . . . 259
East Carlton Park Programme . . . . . . 261
Additional Song Lyrics . . . . . . . 269
Audience Feedback from East Carlton Park . . . . 279
Arc Theatre Programme . . . . . . . 283
MP's Letter of Endorsement . . . . . . 289

AUTHOR'S NOTES

ACT ONE

THE EARLY YEARS

## 1. Labourers from Great Yarmouth
Scene 2, p.15 *Labourers*
Many Labourers who built Corby came from Great Yarmouth in Norfolk, as do the men in this photograph.

## 2. Bevin Boys
p.17 *he was one of the original Bevin Boys*
A recent TV programme showed a campaign to get recognition for the Bevin Boys - or Bevan Boys - who have been derided as conscientious objectors. They played a vital role in the war effort. There is also a debate as to whether they were named after Aneurin Bevan, founder of the NHS, or Ernest Bevin, Minister of Labour and National Service at the time.

The battle to get Black Lung recognised as a disease which Miners suffered from was finally won and a new law was passed in 1979. But for many the battle for compensation continues.

# George gets war recognition at last

## Bevin Boy gets his badge 63 years after ceasefire

■ By Simon Hughes
simon.hughes@northantsnews.co.uk

A CORBY pensioner has finally received recognition for the part he and thousands of other men played in winning the Second World War.

George Ralston received a Bevin Boy Badge through the post yesterday, as a group of 27 former Bevin Boys went to Downing Street for a special presentation ceremony.

Bevin Boy was the name given to miners supplying vital coal during the war and George was thrilled that the day had finally arrived when he and his friends had received recognition.

The 81-year-old, from Burns Drive, in Corby, worked for nearly four years down a mine near Edinburgh after being called up to the service in September 1943.

He said: "I'm delighted because we have tried for so long to get some sort of recognition after we were called up to do National Service.

"I wanted to go into the Army after my twin brother was called up to go, but I received a letter telling me I was going into the coal mines and it was a shock actually.

"I did three years and nine months in the coal mines, and had three close shaves and could have been killed.

"When the letter came saying I had been demobbed it was a great relief to come back to Corby."

The Prime Minister Gordon Brown handed out the badges in a ceremony in London, which commemorated the 60th anniversary of the last Bevin Boy being demobbed, and celebrity Bevin Boys Sir Jimmy Savile and Lord Brian Rix were among those to receive their badge of honour.

Other famous Bevin Boys include the late comedian Eric Morecambe and playwright Peter Shaffer.

Mr Ralston added: "I wasn't one of the lucky ones to be invited to Downing Street, but The Lady Victoria pit near Edinburgh where I worked are having a presentation on May 2 for all the old Bevin Boys, so I hope to attend that."

The Bevin Boys scheme was introduced in 1943 by then Minister for Labour and National Service Ernest Bevin, in response to an increasing shortage of labour in the coal mining industry.

Mr Ralston, who is a member of the 2,000 strong Bevin Boys Association, has always been passionate about their experiences, and in 2005 he published a book called A Bevin Boy's Story.

■ HONOUR – George Ralston

*Evening Telegraph*, 26th March 2008

### 3. Industrial disease and the true cost of Steel

p.17 *Industrial diseases plagued those Working in The Works*
As with Workers in all heavy Industry, the health of those Working in The Works could be severely affected and their life expectancy reduced.

For instance a man who had worked for twenty years as a Steelworker could expect a lifespan of sixty-six years. If he had Worked in the Coke Ovens or the Galvanizing Plant he could expect only fifty-nine years.

*He already had coal dust in his lungs*
In one example a Corby Steelworker, who had been a Miner for years, died without receiving his compensation, as the surgeon who had operated on him refused to sign a form confirming that he had contracted the disease in the Mines. This was despite, years earlier, the same surgeon having vividly described to the family that when she had opened up this man's lungs during an operation, black dust had flown up into her face.

The battle to get diseases caused by Steel dust recognised is still ongoing. John Wood-Cowling, ISTC Executive member at the Steelworks from 1975 to 1981, had an overview of health and safety as part of his role. He told me: "The effects of Steel dust on the lungs can lead to severe bleeding from the nose and throat. It was accepted as an industrial disease in Holland, France and Germany in the 1970s, but is still not recognised here in Britain."

It is the stone dust in the coal which kills Miners, as the coal dust itself dissolves in the lungs. Steel dust, by comparison, does not dissolve. As John said, "Many a layer of Steel dust would be found at the bottom of the bathtub at the end of a Shift as living proof."

Another ex-Steelworker, Andy McCabe, told me of watching the dust settle on his tea if he chose to stay on the Shop Floor for a break.

John told one story of a 42-year-old man Working on the Straightener where the dust could be crushed into black powder. "He started with a heavy nosebleed and was taken off to the ambulance room. A few weeks later he died from severe bleeding to the nose and throat."

Mags McGuire, daughter of a Steelworker, recalled her dad Peter McKay: "He was a Sheet-metal Worker, Tube side, Engineering, and used to have to go in and do repairs during shutdown. He would come home with his scalp scorched where the Red Lead had burned into his head." He died at sixty from lung cancer after years of having been disabled by emphysema.

Another common problem was deafness caused by Working in such noisy conditions. Dennis Taylor, a former Steelworker, remembered Workers from the Rolling Mills not realising they were going deaf, and how they used to shout all the time. He also pointed out that those who Worked with oil to lubricate the Steel or who used it as a coolant would end up with dermatitis. It is now known that prolonged contact with the skin can cause cancer.

Since high-grade asbestos was used to wrap the pipes, asbestosis was also a common occurrence. The following are all illnesses not mentioned so far which are found in higher concentrations amongst Steelworkers:
- Cancer of the bladder and lung
- Heat cataracts
- Pneumonia
- Pneumoconiosis
- Silicosis

If you want to go into this in more detail, the Work and Health Information Gateway www.whig.org.uk carries a copy of Simon Pickvance's *Steelworkers' Handbook*.

## 4. Shift Work

Scene 3, p.24 *Is he on nights?*

The commentator on *Double Harvest* states: "*Continuous production dictates its own terms.*" Indeed this system of Working twenty-one rotating Shifts put great strain on the family.

```
SHIFT ROTA   The 21 shift rota is as follows

             2 days    6 to 2     day   shift
             2 days    10 to 6    night shift
             3 days    2 to 10    back  shift
             2 days    OFF.

             2 days    6 to 2     day   shift
             3 days    10 to 6    night shift
             2 days    2 to 10    back  shift
             2 days    OFF.

             3 days    6 to 2     day   shift
             2 days    10 to 6    night shift
             2 days    2 to 10    back  shift
             3 days    OFF.

             the 3 days off being Friday, Saturday and Sunday.

     NOTE:   Local variations may prevail where the change of shift
             may be at 7 am rather than 6 am.

                                   16
```

One interviewee said: "Whenever Grandad Pop was on Night Shift, it required the family to be silent during the daytime so he could get his head down. Grandma was too busy bringing up the family and looking after the kids to consider Working outside the home."

*I'm up really early so I can sort his feet out*
The wife of a Steelworker would often be awake before her man, preparing his breakfast and making his sandwiches, or "pieces" as they are locally known.

When the Continental Shift system was introduced into Britain in the 1920s, Workers in Presbyterian areas such as Wales and South Yorkshire, backed by their church ministers, refused to Work on a Sunday. The Furnaces were left in safety-only mode until midnight on a Sunday when full production would be resumed.

Eventually a national ballot by the ISTC voted for Continental Shifts to be fully introduced and six-hundred Steelworkers from Sheffield, who refused to co-operate, lost their Jobs.

This Shift pattern was employed within the Blast Furnaces, Coke Ovens and Bi-product Plants and in Steelmaking at the Bessemer, Open Hearth, LD, Electric Furnace, Soaking Pits/Stripping Bay and Rolling Mills.

### A TYPICAL SHIFT ROTA

|        | Mon  | Tue  | Wed  | Thu  | Fri  | Sat  | Sun  |
|--------|------|------|------|------|------|------|------|
| Week 1 | 6-2  | 6-2  | 10-6 | 10-6 | 2-10 | 2-10 | 2-10 |
| Week 2 | OFF  | OFF  | 6-2  | 6-2  | 10-6 | 10-6 | 10-6 |
| Week 3 | 2-10 | 2-10 | OFF  | OFF  | 6-2  | 6-2  | 6-2  |
| Week 4 | 10-6 | 10-6 | 2-10 | 2-10 | OFF  | OFF  | OFF  |

Shifts were:
- Morning Shift        6am - 2pm
- Afternoon ("Back") Shift        2pm - 10pm
- Night Shift        10pm - 6am

The Morgan Mill, which was lighter, ran from 8am - 4pm and 10pm - 6am.

In the Tubes things ran one hour later:
7am - 3pm, 3pm - 11pm and 11pm - 7am.

This was a decision taken in collaboration with the bus company, as it was impossible to deal with both Steelworkers and Tube Workers arriving and leaving together.

The Day Workers Worked 7.30am – 5pm and Office Staff 9am – 5.30pm.

Such overlapping Shifts lend a particular rhythm to the town. The stream of bikes, buses, cars and foot traffic at Shift change-over times is noticeable even now in a town where many Factories still operate these Shifts.

They also play havoc with health and the planning of a social life, and are another contributory factor to the appalling health statistics in the town as a whole.

## 5. Glaswegian dialect
Scene 4, p.29 *We came tae Corby fae Gleasga*
This scene was written in dialect with the help of Spike the Poet, (www.spikepoetry.com). We are aware that there is no standard way to write a Glaswegian dialect, but we hope this will give a flavour of the way Isa spoke.

## 6. Industrial accidents and Workers' Memorial Day
p.30 *he was wan o' the men that fell into the Molten Steel*
The accident mentioned at the heart of this scene was not an isolated incident. During the research one woman reported what she believed to be common practice: that if a man fell into the Molten Steel, the kindest thing to do was to push him under so that he would die more quickly.

What we do know for a fact is that in the early days, deaths at Work were not unusual, due to hazardous Working conditions and lack of regard for the Workers. When John Wood-Cowling first started at The Works in 1963, two Steelworkers per week died in Workplace accidents nationally. Dennis Taylor, some years later, remembers his first day at Work, when a Fitter's Mate fell to his death from thirty feet up in the air.

In the past fifty years there has been huge progress in health and safety in Britain - thanks to dedicated Trade Unionists arguing legislation through, resulting in the Factories Act in 1961 and the Health and Safety at Work Act in 1974. This led to the establishment of the Health and Safety Executive and the formation of organisations such as the Hazards Campaign, a network of resource centres and campaigners on health and safety at Work.

> **The Hazards Campaign is a national network established in 1988, financed by donations from supporting groups and individuals. It draws together hazards centres, occupational health projects, health and safety groups, safety reps networks and Trades Union Councils' Safety Committees, specific campaigns and individual health and safety activists. Specific campaign groups include the Construction Safety Campaign, bereaved relatives' groups, asbestos support groups, RSI support groups, pesticide sufferers' groups, campaigns against hazards affecting Black and ethnic minority groups and toxic waste groups.**
>
> **The campaign works by: sharing information and skills; campaigning on specific issues; acting as a national voice; issuing press releases; holding conferences; establishing national initiatives, including Workers' Memorial Day; lobbying MPs, MEPs and statutory bodies. The Campaign organises the annual Hazards Conference and holds meetings about five times a year which are open to anyone sharing the aims of the campaign.**
>
> **The Hazards Campaign, c/o Greater Manchester Hazards Centre**
> **Windrush Millennium Centre, 70 Alexandra Road, Manchester M16 7WD**
> **www.hazardscampaign.org.uk**

However, every year hundreds of thousands of people still die in Workplace accidents. What causes this and what is left to be done? It seems there are no clear answers.

A young Apprentice Electrician gave his view: "I Work with men who used to Work down The Works. Everyone has their stories of accidents in The Steelworks. One man told me about Contractors being brought in to clear the slag from the

Furnaces and being accidentally blown up by faulty charges; and about Apprentices being crushed by unsecured Machinery or electrocuted by open electrical enclosures. Today there are still employees losing limbs and digits, even under the modern HSE restrictions and guidelines."

Some of these guidelines actually cause other problems. His example: it is no longer permissible to suspend a free-hanging electrical cable from A to B without securing it to avoid anything catching on it. Recently, trying to reach the centre of a cable to secure it (even though there was nothing in sight which could catch on it) required the use of a scissor lift which couldn't reach far enough. The only way to reach it was to undo his harness and lean out of the lift, thereby putting himself at risk. He was reprimanded.

His observation is that in a Unionised Workplace this would not have been a problem, as the Workers still get paid whilst they wait for the Health and Safety Officer to come and assess the situation. However in non-Unionised Workplaces, corners get cut and the pressure is on to finish the Job.

Also genuine accidents happen with the best will in the world, like when his colleague's Stanley knife slipped out of a secured harness as they were crawling along a gantry thirty feet up in the air. It narrowly avoided hitting someone. All the Workers from his firm were thrown off site as a result.

Speaking to Health and Safety officers, three problems were identified. One was that financial constraints mean that corners get cut to get a Job done quicker. Following the guidelines properly may add time to a Job. Employers have to abide by government legislation to avoid legal action, but they try to get round it whenever they can. In addition good quality Health and Safety equipment costs money and is one of the first areas where savings are made. Secondly, there is a macho Work culture based on risk-taking. And thirdly there is an increasing safety awareness issue for Workers for whom English is a second language, and those who speak enough English to get by, but who do not read it. This is not a new problem.

As we point out at various times in the play, Corby has always had a rich ethnic mix. John Wood-Cowling remembers attending a death at the Steelworks in the 1960s, where a Ukrainian Worker had been crushed by a Crane in the Basic Oxygen Plant. His widow got compensation, because she explained that he would have been unable to read the text on the safety notice - which failed to show the universally-recognised danger symbol of a skull and crossbones.

It is imperative that the government reinstate funding to provide free ESOL classes in the Workplace. They argue that the employer should bear this responsibility, but there is much evidence to show that this is not the case.

One point on which both sides agree is the Hard Hat battle. The HSOs acknowledge that they are often uncomfortable or impractical. A young Fencer said that they must have been designed by "the bods who wear them for half an hour to inspect the site but don't have to Work in them". He gave this example: attaching fencing to the top floor of a multi-storey car park required him to lean over the edge. He knew his Hat would fall off. Since there was only the sky above him he decided to take his Hat off to complete the Job. When ordered to put it back on by the HSO, just as predicted the Hat fell off - risking causing injury to someone below, as it fell thirty feet to the ground.

The HSO's response in this case was: "Try telling his widow, if he had fallen to the ground and died from a head injury, why he was not made to wear his Hat."

The Health and Safety seesaw will continue. Hopefully the more Unionised Workplaces there are, the less financial pressure there will be to cut corners. But where there are huge sums of money involved, getting a Job completed within the given timescale will always create dangerous pressure.

Finally an anecdote about real danger at Work from this same young man was how he narrowly avoided being attacked by a tiger whilst fencing at Woburn Safari Park. He pointed out that this "kind of put things into perspective".

Workers who are killed in the Workplace are commemorated annually on 28th April, International Workers' Memorial Day. In Corby, after attending the Hazards Conference in September 1997, the late Davy Williamson of the General Municipal and Boilermakers' Union campaigned for our own Memorial to Workers who died at Work. The original plaque was placed in Coronation Park and a second one was later added to the Steelworker Statue.

Gordon Glassford, Secretary of the GMB, told me: "We have held a gathering at the plaque every year since 1998 on the Saturday nearest to Workers' Memorial Day. We observe a minute's silence at eleven o'clock and remember those who have died at Work."

EVENING TELEGRAPH

## Memorial tribute to workers

WORKERS have been remembered in a memorial day tribute.

Corby mayor Jimmy Noble unveiled a stone plaque and a tree was planted in Coronation Park, Corby, to recognise all the people who have died at work or travelling to and from work.

The event was part of Workers' Memorial Day, which is on April 28 each year.

Events in Britain were organised by the GMB union and included campaigning for improved working conditions.

Mr Noble said: "It was well organised and nice of the GMB union to recognise Workers' Memorial Day. It started a few years ago in America and we have continued it in the UK.

"It was never really appreciated in Corby so it was interesting to see the GMB come up with the idea. Hopefully we can continue it and do something on the anniversary every year."

More than 8,000 workers die in the UK each year from work related diseases and accidents.

The vast majority of these deaths are connected with diseases caused by exposure to asbestos and other dusts.

■ UNVEILED – Corby mayor Jimmy Noble kneels beside the plaque watched by councillors and GMB members

### 7. Women in the Steel Industry

Scene 5, p.33 *I was the youngest woman in the Steelworks*

During the war Corby women were employed in The Works. Some Worked on constructing the pipeline under the ocean known as PLUTO. Two of these women, Winnie Scott and Jean Hall, can be heard telling their stories on the *Women of Steel* CD.

This article shows Michael Leahy from the Trade Union Community (formerly the ISTC), presenting them with an award.

## Honour for two Corby women pioneers

*Two proud pioneers: Winnie and Jean with Community Union General Secretary Michael Leahy who presented the statues of a Steelworker.*

**Two Corby women have been honoured** for their ground-breaking work on a special project at Corby Steelworks during the second world war. Winnie Scott and Jean Hall were honoured by the trade union Community (formerly the ISTC) for their part in the PLUTO Project (Pipe Line Under The Ocean). The pipeline enabled fuel supplies to be delivered to France for the D-Day landings in June 1944. Winnie and Jean were presented with a statue of a Steelworker by Community general secretary Michael Leahy who said that the two Corby women are believed to be among the first women ever to work in the British Steel Industry. Explaining the change in the union's name, Michael Leahy said that Community now organised not only people in Steel but in many other industries and businesses in Steel areas. "Community has particularly strong links with Corby", he said, "and we are determined to offer the benefits of union membership to all those who need it in the town."

Unfortunately, the PLUTO pub on Gainsborough Road, the one public building which recalled this important contribution to the war effort, has recently been demolished. Though the building had fallen into disrepair, I hope some other civic building will carry on the story. However, there are plans to erect a plaque to honour the PLUTO women.

*We women were all being paid off, like after the war*
In Corby, some women were retained as Crane Drivers. In Rotherham, where Rolled and Razor-blade Steel was made, up to 80% of the Workforce were women.

## 8. Estate renewal, compulsory removal, or time to move on
p.41 *But I've raised my family here, it's where I live, it's my home*
In 2007, as part of a major redevelopment project, after months of consultation and negotiation, a large part of Lincoln Way was demolished.

Where did the people go? How did it feel to be served a Notice of Demolition?

For some, this was a step up, a chance to move off what is often considered to be a failing estate. But other people asked to be moved to a different house on the same estate! Why? Some very human reasons:

One woman was caring for her friend in the last stages of cancer, and would have been unable to do so if she had moved to another area. She, in effect, forfeited the opportunity to get off the estate in an act of selflessness typical on this "worst estate".

The oldest person to be moved was ninety-two and she too wanted to stay close by her support networks.

One man did not want to leave the memories of his wife who had died in the house. With hindsight, moving house has helped him move on emotionally.

For many there was a financial incentive in the package that the council offered to those tenants being required to relocate:
- A move to another like-for-like house in their chosen area
- £4,400 Home Loss payment
- Removals arranged and paid for by CBC
- Reimbursements for utilities, new satellite dishes etc.

With homeowners the story was a bit different. They were offered the market value of their property plus 10%. Sounds like a good deal, but obviously a three-bed property on the "worst estate" is not comparable to one elsewhere!

And as one ex-resident remarked, a move to a "better" area means that she is no longer comfortable to walk the dog in her pyjamas - another reference to that same community spirit mentioned in Maureen's story!

It must be noted that this process was not confined to the Kingswood estate and was part of the regeneration of Arran Way. It would seem that unfortunately, in the name of regeneration, established communities have been splintered.

### 9. Works social
Scene 7, p.54 *Workers in the Canteen enjoying a social*
Irene, who provided us with this photo for the play, writes: "This picture Worked as a slide to suggest a Works social, but it is of my Auntie Jean, who died in 1976 aged over seventy, and her cronies - probably taken in another Canteen years earlier than 1974 when this piece is set."

### 10. As The Works Grows
p.57 *SONG: AS THE WORKS GROWS, SO THE TOWN GROWS*
This scene was originally designed by Lyn, Jan and Lola as a three-minute audio-visual piece to be played in the cinema area of the Steel Heritage Centre during the promenade performance in 2006.

However, the soundproofing between the rooms was inadequate, so instead the song was performed live in the café area with the images projected on screen. The audio-visual version was used at the Arc.

We decided to present this scene as a photo-montage version in the book.

### 11. Corby New Town in its heyday
Scene 8, p.65 *This purely visual scene*
In the process of compiling the book it was necessary to source many of the originals of the images used in the visual script. In doing so, Kenneth unearthed so many wonderful photos of Old Corby that we decided to include a purely photographic chapter which celebrates Corby in its heyday.

### 12. Closure announced
Scene 9, p.73 *In February 1979, British Steel announced plans to close the Steel end of the Corby Plant*

## Time-line for the Closure of the Steelworks in Corby

**February 1979**
With 5,500 jobs under threat it emerges there are just 60 job vacancies at the Job Centre.

Steelworkers and their families lobby then Tory-controlled Corby Council in protest at being charged for action committee meetings at the Festival Hall.

The council is accused of not doing enough to stop the closure, despite sending a delegation to the government.

**April 1979**
Mass rally held at the Festival Hall organised by ROSAC – the campaign for the Retention Of Steelmaking At Corby.

Total job losses predicted to be as many as 12,000.

**June 1979**
Thirty steelworkers and union leaders, including former council chairman Peter McGowan and former Mayor John Wood-Cowling set off on an 80-mile Jarrow-style crusade to London.

Six days later, they were joined by 400 people and travelled down from Corby for a rally around central London and a 10,000 signature petition was handed in to the House of Commons.

At the Iron and Steel Trades Confederation (ISTC) British Steel boss Sir Charles Villiers gives the clearest hint that nothing will stop the axe form falling.

Corby people feature in a documentary about how the closure will affect their lives.

A huge illuminated Save Our Steel sign is erected on top of the Strathclyde Hotel.

**July 1979**
British Steel challenges union bosses to come up cash saving ideas as an alternative to closure.

Corby Council appoints a jobs supremo, charged with attracting new jobs to the town.

The new Tory government, led by Margaret Thatcher, promises to keep a close eye on the negotiations.

**August 1979**
Shadow industry secretary John Silkin visits Corby on a fact finding mission.

A Corby delegation meets former Labour premier Jim Callaghan in London.

### September 1979
Talks between British Steel and the ISTC in Corby are disrupted by 10,000 people taking to the streets.

There are scuffles between protestors and the police. No arrests were made.

### October 1979
One thousand extra police are drafted in as Corby readies itself for the expected closure announcement on November 1st.

British Steel has urgent talks with the government claiming the corporation is losing 10m a week.

### November 1979
Announcement made that the steel works will close in a year's time. Corby Council applies to the government and the EEC for grants. Eventually £300m is given.

ISTC and other unions vow to continue their fight against closure.

### December 1979
British Steel offers steelworkers a 2% pay rise, which eventually leads to a national strike.

Splits between union members begin to appear. Two thousand engineers vote for shutdown and a decent redundancy package, as do about 1,200 blast furnacemen. 6,000 ISTC members accept the inevitable closure.

### January 1980
National steel strike over pay begins, but some Corby workers turn up for work, anxious not to jeopardise redundancy pay.

### February 1980
Glebe coke ovens close. Seven hundred maintenance workers let go and 1,500 workers from the minerals and preparation plant and a major blast furnace are given notice.

National strike continues.

### March 1980
The average Corby family is living on £24 a week. Blast furnacemen demand answers about strike pay, but there are clashes with strike supporters outside the Festival Hall.

### April 1980
Twelve week strike ends as steelmakers accept 15.5% pay offer.

Redundancies were phased throughout 1980.

The last steel was made on April 22nd.

This news sent shock waves across the community.

These are two verses written by a Steelworker at the time.

(S.O.T? = SAVE OUR TOWN

This is a national disaster, that everyone will feel
When the new town of Corby, loses its steel
No more will the people, hear the furnaces roar
For the workers of Stewart & Lloyds, will be out the door

You can overhear conversations, and people mutter
What will become of us, we can't earn our bread & butter.
The people of Corby, won't know, what way to turn
For Corby will be a ghost town, with no candle to burn?

A solution must be found, and very quick friend
For if not found, for Corby, it will be the end.
Is this the thanks we get? for our sweat and guts
Living in Briqstock Camp, in those filthy huts.

The workers in Corby, made S & L what it was
Now after all the years of toil, its a lost cause?
The workers in Corby, don't want any handouts or gratuities
Most of all they don't want, is to be on Social Security?

So dear steel bosses, and management, don't just sit & sigh
Or else it will be the end, and Corby will surely die
All I can say to the Corby workers is, for you to unite
Don't sacrifice your lovely town, without a damn good
                                                    FIGHT

With one in five townsfolk employed in The Works, the potential impact of Closure was massive. Other Jobs were related indirectly to the Steel Industry, and they too would be lost if The Works closed.

> **HAVE - FAITH ?**
>
> MY JEANS WORKS IN STEWART & LLOYDS AS A CLEANER IN STEEL-SIDE
> ALL THE WORKERS THERE, ARE BEEN TAKING FOR A RIDE ?
> NO MORE WILL FURNACES ROAR, OR GIANT POTS BE FILLED
> FOR CORBY STEEL SIDE, WILL SURELY-BE, JUST KILLED
>
> THE PEOPLE OF CORBY LOOK GRIM, AND FEEL-SO DEPRESSED
> THE NUMBER OF THOSE REDUNDANT, HAS BEEN ASSESSED ?
> PEOPLE IN CORBY ARE WORRIED, AND AT THEIR WITS-END
> WITH THE THOUGHT OF NO CASH, ITS ENOUGH TO DRIVE YOU ROUND THE BEND
>
> HOW CAN CORBY SURVIVE, OR PEOPLE PAY THEIR HOUSE-RENTS
> THEY WILL BECOME LIKE NOMADS, AND HAVE TO LIVE IN TENTS
> NOW CORBY WITH NO MORE STEEL TO TAP
> WILL JUST DISSAPEAR OFF THE BLINKING MAP ?
>
> NOW THE UNION'S SAY NOT TO WORRY, WELL THINK UP SOMETHING GOOD
> BUT IF THERE'S NO JOBS, THEY'LL BE NO MONEY FOR RENT OR FOOD
>
> THE UNIONS SAY THEY STILL HAVE GOT A HOT TIP
> THEY START TO PREACH ABOUT THE MICRO-CHIP
> THE ONLY THING TO DO IS PRAY TO GOD HE IS GOOD
> HE WILL NOT SEE US SUFFER OR GO WITHOUT FOOD
> SO DON'T WORRY CORBY OUR LORD WILL NOT LET YOU-DOWN
> HE WILL THINK OF SOMETHING TO SAVE OUR CORBY-TOWN

There were far-sighted people in the town who had tried to diversify Corby's employment base for years, to avoid such a disaster. But they had had little success, as Corby was very much a one-horse town.

## 13. ROSAC
*p.73 The newly-formed campaign group ROSAC*
This chapter includes additional photos of the many Actions there were to Save the Steelworks. We felt it was important to honour the tremendous fight put up by the people of Corby, and to let this archive material be seen.

# STEELFIGHT news
### AUGUST 1979
**free**

PUBLISHED BY R.O.S.A.C. (RETENTION OF STEELMAKING AT CORBY) No. 5

**r.o.s.a.c.** R.O.S.A.C. IS A BROADLY-BASED, NON-POLITICAL, COMMUNITY ORGANISATION DEDICATED TO THE CONTINUANCE OF STEEL-MAKING AT CORBY IN THE SURE KNOWLEDGE THAT THE END OF STEELMAKING WOULD MEAN THE DEATH OF A WHOLE NEW TOWN, ITS COMMUNITY LIFE, ITS SCHOOLS, BUSINESSES, JOBS; IT WOULD MEAN NO REAL FUTURE FOR YOUNG PEOPLE.

ONCE AGAIN R.O.S.A.C IS PUBLISHING STEELFIGHT NEWS, IN RESPONSE TO POPULAR DEMAND. WE HAVE BEEN PUBLISHING LEAFLETS ON SPECIAL ISSUES AND WE SHALL CONTINUE TO DO SO AGAIN, SOON. IF YOU HAVE ANY NEWS OR VIEWS OR SPECIAL BITS OF INFORMATION YOU'D LIKE PUBLISHING THEN LET US KNOW AT THE R.O.S.A.C. OFFICE.

ON JUNE 21ST CHARLES VILLIERS, B.S.C. SUPREMO, SAID "CLOSURE AT CORBY IS CERTAIN AND THE TOWN WOULD HAVE TO GET USED TO THE FACT". SIR CHARLES IS NOW GETTING USED TO THE FACT THAT WE WILL NOT GIVE IN MEEKLY AND THAT CORBY IS FIGHTING.

LED BY R.O.S.A.C., THE CAMPAIGN HAS GAINED STRENGTH FAR EXCEEDING THE HOPES OF EVEN THE STAUNCHEST FIGHTERS. THE PLAN WAS TO AXE SOME 7,000 JOBS FROM CORBY AND TO STRIKE AT THE HEART OF THE COMMUNITY. BUT THE CORBY-LONDON MARCH, WITH ITS TREMENDOUS SUPPORT FROM THE TOWNS-PEOPLE AND FAMILIES, CUT DEEPLY INTO THE B.S.C.'S ARROGANCE.

THE JULY 12TH LOBBY OF B.S.C. HEADQUARTERS IN LONDON'S GROSVENOR PLACE (COMPLETE WITH FLAG) - THE OPEN DOOR PROGRAMME - AND AN ABSOLUTELY TREMENDOUS SHOW OF STRENGTH IN THE 6,000 STRONG DEMONSTRATION FROM THE WORKS TO THE CIVIC CENTRE ON JULY 20TH, INTENSIFIED THE CAMPAIGN.

HUGE CRACKS ARE NOW APPEARING IN B.S.C'S CASE. WE HAVEN'T WON YET BUT DOUBTS ABOUT OUR ABILITY TO FIGHT HAVE BEEN DISPELLED.

THE LATEST NEWS THIS WEEK IS THAT THE THATCHER(MIS)GOVERNMENT HAS THE SUPREME CHEEK TO TRY TO BRIBE THE TOWN'S CIVIC LEADERS WITH A PALTRY THREE-MILLION QUID - MONEY WHICH HAD ALREADY BEEN OFFERED TO THE DEVELOPMENT CORPORATION ANYWAY FOR CONSOLIDATION OF LAND ON WHICH TO BUILD FACTORIES.

THE THREE-MILLION QUID WOULD ALSO APPEAR TO HAVE STRINGS TO IT AND THE OFFER OF ASSISTED-AREA STATUS IS ALSO CONDITIONAL ON THE CLOSURE OF THE STEELWORKS. BUT EVEN THEN IT IS ONLY A POSSIBILITY-NOT A FIRM OFFER.

WHAT SORT OF PEOPLE DO THEY THINK WE ARE IN CORBY? THEY OBVIOUSLY THINK THAT ANYBODY CAN BE BOUGHT FOR A MERE PITANCE. WE'LL HAVE TO ENCOURAGE THEM TO HAVE ANOTHER THINK! THIS TOWN IS WORTH FIGHTING FOR!

## thanks, folks!

R.O.S.A.C thanks especially the Strathclyde Hotel for its continuing support, Corby Motors for free van-loan on the Corby-London Walk, Studfall Hairdresser and many others for their their help - not forgetting B.S.C. for steel tubing and the Phantom Painters who continue to STRIKE fear into the heart of a certain Harry Ford.

## help?

Since the Walk to London and Rally from Hyde Park to House of Commons, and the OPEN DOOR TV programme people from all over Corby are coming forward with offers of help- teachers, social workers, youth and community staff, trade unionists outside the works and many of the public at large are willing to help and are wanting information on the campaign. If you want to help or need information then call at R.O.S.A.C.'s new office in the Festival Hall Foyer, tel. Corby 2551.

## new office

R.O.S.A.C.'s new Office has been made generously available by Corby District Council and it will help greatly to centralise the information role of R.O.S.A.C.
It will also give us a more public face and improve public relations. We hope that the office will be open every day until after the Festival Against Closure on August 18, and permanently after that.

## banner

A team from Birmingham's Banner Theatre will be working in Corby soon. They will be collecting material for a show about Corby and its steel problems, So, they would like to meet as many people as possible and to taperecord their memories, songs, stories and their attitudes to steel closures. Watch out for further details but, again, if you would like to help on an exciting project then call at R.O.S.A.C. office and tell us.

## dirty tricks dept.

As warned by speakers at the July 20th mass meeting, B.S.C. has already started a programme to undermine R.O.S.A.C.'s campaign.

1. What about the speedy reline of No 1. furnace?
2. Why did the Glebe Coke Ovens close down permanantly?
3. Who authorised the special steel strip trains from Lackenby?

R.O.S.A.C. urges all B.S.C. employees to remain vigilant and to ensure that no more dirty tricks will happen.

## festival

Following previous successful demonstrations, Walk to London, Rallys, Public Meetings, etc. R.O.S.A.C. is now planning a major FESTIVAL AGAINST CLOSURE., for August 18th. in the CIVIC CENTRE SQUARE. It will be an event for the whole community and a chance to show once again that Corby means business, It's also a chance to show solidarity in the fight against B.S.C. and to have a good time into the bargain. It will run from mid-morning with a march from Studfall to Town until late evening with a Dance-Cabaret in the Festival Hall. There really will be something for everybody - openlair Party for the kids, stalls, films, exhbitions, clowns, singers, bands, bars, Rally with national figures speaking in support of Corby's fight against Town Murder by B.S.C. There will also be continuous showings of the R.O.S.A.C.-B.B.C. OPEN DOOR programme.

## support

During the last few weeks R.O.S.A.C. has received many hundreds of letters of support from all over the country and people have sent donations of almost fourhundred pounds. It is obvious that people really care about us for they have written to M.P.s and the Government on our behalf. They have sent poems, songs, and have bought our badges, car stickers, T-shirts, posters, have taken thousands of our leaflets so that they can spread spread the R.O.S.A.C. message throughout the country.

## r.o.s.a.c. stall

Don't forget to come and support us at the R.O.S.A.C. stall in Corby Market Square every Saturday morning. Identify yourself with us! Talk to us about the campaign! Findout about the forthcoming activities in which we know you will wish to take part! And we need helpers to keep the stall open for the whole of Saturday - not just the morning!

## open door

R.O.S.A.C.'s highly commended OPEN DOOR tv programme is now available on Video Cassette for public showing. If you and your organisation would like a showing and a speaker from R.O.S.A.C. then let us know as soon as possible. We have a large panel of experts who will be more than pleased to come along to explain the details of our campaign against the British Steel Corporation. Help to save Corby - organise a meeting !

DON'T FORGET - R.O.S.A.C. NEEDS CASH TO CONTINUE THE STRUGGLE. ANYTHING YOU CAN AFFORD OR CAN COLLECT WILL BE VERY WELCOME.

## 14. The Strike

p.75 *So ladies, all those in favour of supporting the Strike...*
As this scene shows, not everyone was unanimous in support of the Strike. Picket Lines were set up to try to dissuade those not yet convinced. Karen, as the ISTC Rep, had the Job of persuading her members to strike: *"I'm counting on you to come out and make this a solid response."*

But there were a lot of Unions at The Works and they did not all come out together, if at all. On the first day of the Strike, Ann-Marie Lawson, an Office Worker on the Picket Line, ended up smashing her own car window to stop her husband, who was in the AUEW Union that had not yet come out, from crossing the Picket Line. "There was no way I could let him be a scab! Even if it did cost us a new windscreen!"

Another story, from John Wood-Cowling, in his own words: "During the strike we had about thirty women crossed the Picket Line - Office Workers. We had an American, Louis Gadke, a serviceman who married a local girl. Louis came up with a plan: a Mexican Picket. The police always covered the gate in the morning but didn't bother when the women left at night, so Louis and the lads refused to allow them to go home!

Needless to say, the hard-pressed police advised them: 'Ladies, stay at home. You're more bother than you're worth'. This was the first time a Mexican Picket was ever used in the UK; it was adopted by many other Unions later. It was first used by Mexican Fruit Packers in California."

## 15. Policing

p.86 *Remember this was 1979, before Greenham Common and the Miners' Strike. Before police in riot gear were a common sight.*
Between the Steel Strike and the Miners' Strike we witnessed the increasing militarisation of the police force, who were used politically and violently to suppress Strikes and other popular Protests, like the peace movement, throughout the 1980s.

It may be worth pointing out that the police received massive inflation-busting pay awards during the 1980s. Also it has been well documented that many army personnel, e.g. SAS and Paras, were seen in police uniforms at many disputes, as well as acting as *agents provocateurs*, deliberately posing as Protestors and instigating violence towards the police to give an excuse for retaliation.

As both an Activist and a Legal Observer at various Non-Violent Direct Actions during the 1980s, I was often hampered in my task of noting the number of the arresting officer because they would remove their identification numbers. Their tactics became increasingly brutal.

The most sickening for me was the sight of a charge of police horses towards a peaceful Blockade of women at Greenham Common in 1982. Amazingly enough, one woman shouted to the others to lie flat, something she had seen in the film *Gandhi* where a similar thing had happened. The horses reared and refused to trample on the prone bodies of the frightened women.

And where was the famous "free British press" during these events? At Greenham, almost overnight, after April 1985 the media stopped reporting what was happening from both sides. Those in the movement believe to this day that this was politically controlled.

Yes, this was the era of "the enemy within", a particularly offensive label that Maggie Thatcher first used to describe the Striking Miners in 1984. As a concept it was subsequently applied to anyone who dared stand against the government.

The use of roadblocks to prevent Flying Pickets moving from Pit to Pit during the Miners' Strike was another tactic employed by the police under instruction from the government. It was a further sinister erosion of our Civil Liberties. The car in which I was travelling on the way back from the Peak District in 1984 was stopped at one such roadblock, and we were turned back under suspicion of being en route to a Picket Line.

Lasting damage was done to communities who were on the receiving end of this political policing. The very people that we are meant to trust to keep us safe are seen as being on the other side.

Monitoring of police behaviour became a necessity.

On 6th February 1985, the community living on Molesworth Airbase and cultivating the land to grow wheat to send to the starving people of Eritrea was evicted overnight. Michael Heseltine, the then Minister of Defence, deployed fifteen hundred police and troops to the site to secure the base for the MOD. This was the single largest mobilisation of police and troops since World War II. For the Royal Engineers it was their largest operation since the bridging of the Rhine in 1944.

The evicted residents made their way to land near Corby. Supporters in the town tried to help the evicted residents, and were so appalled at the behaviour of the local police that we formed the Corby Police Watch Committee to closely monitor Civil Liberties.

Molesworth subsequently became the second USAAF base to house Cruise missiles (US nuclear weapons), with lively Protests, well-supported by Corby CND and Wimmin For Peace throughout the late 1980s.

I found the swoop arrests at Molesworth particularly ominous. Police in riot gear would suddenly put on their gloves, get tooled up and head off towards random Protestors, who would be dragged unceremoniously back to the waiting police van. Intimidation and violence were deliberate tactics used to scare off the faint-hearted.

Militarised police behaviour was in evidence at the eleventh-hour demonstration outside Parliament in 1991 on the eve of the outbreak of the first Gulf War. Thousands of Protestors had gathered to hold a candlelit Vigil to try to persuade the government to pull back from the brink of war and to actively say "Not in my name."

I was outside the Foreign Office and about to leave. I climbed on a wall to see how many people there were. I saw the police lines moving in, clearly with the intention of blocking in the Protestors from three sides, leaving only one escape route. Being on the wall saved me from being trampled.

By the time of the Dockers' Strike in 1995, riot police had gone through various developments. The special patrol group (SPG), suspected of killing Anti-Nazi League member Blair Peach on a demonstration in 1979, was disbanded in 1987. They were replaced by the territorial support group (TSG). The speed and severity of their response was terrifying. I was on the Picket Line at Seaforth Docks on the first anniversary of the Strike, when a group of Protestors, pretending to leave the Protest, actually managed to get through the fence, leaving the way for others to get onto the premises.

I will never forget the sight of the TSG pulling down their visors and grabbing their batons, which ironically had been made in Northamptonshire. They looked like they were chasing hardened criminals who they expected to be armed, rather than a bunch of unarmed peaceful Protestors. Watching them randomly baton someone to the ground was horrible.

I had become well acquainted with these particular batons and their correct use, as I had just finished playing a police officer in Banner Theatre's production *Criminal Justice*. The role required me to demonstrate their correct usage every night of the tour! The play had used the recently-passed Criminal Justice Act as a starting point to examine the slow but sure erosion of our Civil Liberties, pointing out how much that had been tried and tested in the battleground of Northern Ireland was becoming part of English law.

How are things nowadays?

When protesting in Scotland in 2007 against Trident nuclear submarines, No Nukes Northants had a largely positive experience of the police.

Having trained people up to expect the sort of violent and militarised policing described above, it was a shock to the system to be treated courteously by officers simply upholding the law of the land. Many of the officers agreed with our point of view, but individual conscience alone cannot account for this change in tactics. Maybe lessons have been learned, or maybe a Labour government does not seek to exert political control over the police force. Or maybe it is different in Scotland, since tales of police brutality at the Protests against the third runway at Heathrow in summer 2007 are all too common.

The slow, steady erosion of our hard-won Civil Liberties continues, even under a Labour government. In the name of tightened security as part of the "war on terror", our right to peaceful Protest is being taken away.

In 2005 the Serious and Organised Crime and Police Act was passed. This act bans people from demonstrating in any area designated by the government. One of these "designated areas" is the square kilometre around Parliament.

This measure was a crude attempt to get rid of peace campaigner Brian Haw, who set up a permanent camp opposite the Houses of Parliament in protest at the Iraq War in 2001 (see www.parliament-square.org.uk).

However only this week, 27th March 2008, the newspapers reported that the right to protest outside Parliament is to be restored, two years after the government banned it.

In conclusion, we must never take our hard-won rights for granted. Be vigilant. We live in a democratic country. Do not be afraid to exercise your right of free speech.

## 16. The Steel Strike in context: Trade Union history
Scene 11, p.94 *Steel is dead. Who wants to work in heavy industry?*
I wanted to place the Steel Strike in the context of Maggie Thatcher's intentional and systematic destruction of the Trade Union Movement.

John Wood-Cowling explained: "Let us not forget that it was a Labour minister, Eric Varley, as part of a Labour government, who gave the go-ahead for Closure of the Steelworks in 1979.

"The Labour government had been advised to reduce the number of both Steelworks and Coal Mines, and replace them with supermines. This was the situation Maggie Thatcher inherited when she came to power. She and her right-wing think tank knew that the combined power of the three big Industrial Unions - Steel, Coal and Rail - could destroy the economy. They formulated a plan to limit this potential power."

The systematic destruction of first the Steel Industry and then the Coal Mining Industry was all part of this plan. The breaking of the Unions and the introduction of anti-Trade Union legislation effectively wiped out the hard-won gains of 150 years.

Since the formation of the first Trade Union by the momentous actions of the 'Tolpuddle Martyrs' (see www.tolpuddlemartyrs.org.uk) in 1833, to the present day, the right to withdraw one's Labour in protest at unfair pay and conditions is part and parcel of any democratic industrialised nation. But Maggie had other plans.

John takes up the story: "The tories decided to starve out the Steelworkers and break the Union. With inflation running at 16%, Steelworkers were offered a shocking 2% pay rise. There was evidence that British Steel Corporation were stockpiling and were keen for the men to Strike."

The Steelworkers held out for three months, and five years later the Miners held out for a year.

And of course let us not forget the Wapping Dispute in 1986, which was notoriously used to break the Print Workers' organisation. It was won by the government through the use of very repressive policing, including restricting the movement of local residents and making 1000 arrests. In addition scabs were taken to and from Work in specially-reinforced buses.

So what became of the Rail Union? The privatisation of the railways was, in my opinion, less to do with improving efficiency than it was to do with attempting to break up this powerful Union. However, as Trade Unionist Sean Kettle pointed out, this failed:

"In fact the Rail Union RMT, under the stewardship of the late Jimmy Knapp and now Bob Crowe, is one of the few Unions who continue to report year-by-year increase in membership simply because they campaign vigorously on behalf of their members. Crowe is now receiving the same kind of vilification as Arthur Scargill did when he was NUM (National Union of Miners) President.

"Personally I think the Rail privatisation was about allowing their friends in the city to get their greedy snouts in the cash trough. I saw the same happen in the Water Industry."

## 17. Demolition

p.96 *Images on the screen detailing the demolition of The Steelworks*

Many people shared their emotional memories with me about watching the demolition. Large crowds gathered to do so. Charlie Connor, now a bus driver, was nine at the time, a pupil at Our Lady's School on Occupation Road. Ten minutes before demolition of the Cooling Towers, his teacher, Mrs Lennon, told the children to go and look out of the windows. He remembers feeling the rumble from where they stood. He said: "We knew it was the end of The Works. We'd followed the marches and would run home to watch them on the news."

Kenneth added: "My mum took three photographs on her old Kodak instamatic camera that shows the Gasometer coming down in August 1980 (pictured right). Sitting in the foreground are myself and my two brothers - William and Graham; along with our cousin Daniel Parvin, who was visiting from Derbyshire. I was aged six at the time and recall the sound of the crash but to be honest I was a bit too young to absorb the real impact this would later have upon the town. I was more interested in playing with my toy cars, as can be seen from my lack of attention on the demolition. Brother William (far right) seems to be the only one who was taking any notice."

The clean-up process after demolition was very poor, and there is a lasting legacy of toxic waste. Some still argue that this is the cause of the high number of births of children who have limbs or fingers missing.

---

**Council sets aside £200,000 to fight toxic waste case**

A COUNCIL has put aside £200,000 of taxpayers' money to fight a toxic waste compensation claim. Corby Council has earmarked cash from its reserves to cover legal expenses in defending the action being lodged by more than 20 families.

The group says harmful toxins escaped during the reclamation of land contaminated by the town's former steel works between 1986 and 1999, which it says caused birth defects.

The council has always said it will fight the claims and has not admitted liability.

Source: Evening Telegraph
Date : 29/11/2005

# ACT TWO

# STAND YOUR GROUND

## 18. Banner Theatre
Scene 2, p.111 *SONG: BROKEN DREAMS*
This is the first of two songs written by Dave Rogers from Banner Theatre. The other one is *Sweatshop* in Act Two Scene 4. Both these songs are from the 1994 production *Sweatshop*. The play examined the position of Workers in the global economy, and research for this production was partly carried out in Corby.

Birmingham-based Banner Theatre are the longest-standing political theatre company in England. They wrote a play called *Steel* at the time of the Strike and have always retained their link with the town.

I toured as a member of the company from 1994 to 1998 and furthered my documentary drama skills enormously through being part of researching, creating and performing in *Sweatshop, Criminal Justice, Redemption Song* and *Free for All*. Sami Scott, our Technician, also trained and Worked with Banner. For more information about Banner Theatre visit: www.bannertheatre.co.uk

## 19. Working Class women speak out
Scene 3, p.113 *So we better practise what we want to say!*
These monologues from the Women of Steel deal with the core issues of Redundancy, and would have been the sort of tales they told when visiting the Miners' Wives to share their experiences and give support.

This scene was inspired by the powerful speeches which I heard during both the 1984 Miners' Strike and the 1995 Dockers' Strike. Women from those communities went on speaking tours to raise support, as had the women at Greenham Common before them. Moving heartfelt testimonies without a hint of the false spin of polished professional speechwriters.

For many women this was a first step into the public arena, and although initially terrifying, it often proved to be ultimately very empowering. In 1984 I had the honour of sharing a platform with a Miner's Wife from Nottingham at a benefit gig in Holland. I acted as translator when her broad accent proved to be too much for the Dutch audience, who normally would have understood English!

And then during the *Redemption Song* tour with Banner Theatre in 1997, I got to know the Women of the Waterfront whose voices we recorded for our CD. This is an excerpt from a letter put together to try and boost the numbers of their group, by Doreen McNally, a particularly eloquent Woman of the Waterfront:

"The vast majority of us have never before belonged to an organised group of this nature, even those of us who are committee members. Most of us have led our lives on the sidelines, bringing up our families and holding down our Jobs. Our men, and probably yours, were happy for us to remain away from the action while they, with the help of the Stewards, fought for reinstatement. They were too proud to ask for help. However, we saw the need to face facts: that we must all play our part to end this awful situation. Some of us have managed to go outside of Merseyside and have been amazed and humbled to find the esteem in which Liverpool Dockers are held. We firmly believe that we'll win this fight because morality and human decency are on our side. Victory will come all the sooner if you demonstrate that you are too."

## 20. Workers' Rights Group
p.115 *the Workers' Rights Group is leafleting*
I have used artistic licence in this scene which is set in 1984. The WRG was not set up until 1986. The group began fundraising for a van which would go to the gates of the new Factories on the Earlstrees Industrial Estate, many of which were non-Unionised, in order to inform people of their employment rights.

As we hear in this monologue, there were many fly-by-night employers taking advantage of rate-free premises and the surplus of Labour in the wake of the Closure of The Works.

Although the group raised funds easily to begin with, they never got enough for the van. Instead they opened a drop-in session and phone line from an office in the Labour Club advertised in the local *Evening Telegraph*.

The group was made up of Trade Unionists representing blue and white-collar Workers. It was supported by and reported to the Trades Council, and received a lot of support from Labour Party branch members.

I would personally like to mention some of the Activists who ran this group, as we often forget to thank those Comrades who try to make a difference. Many of them were also active in the Trades Council which did a lot to try and improve conditions for Workers generally in the town.

Elaine Barker, Willy Barr, Tommie Beattie, Tim Cunningham, Pete Currall, Gary Doherty, Alan Irwin and John Reilly all played a part.

## 21. Trade Unions today

p.115 *The Union was a way of life down The Works...Now it is everyone for themselves...Divide and rule.*

That was in 1985. How do things stand today, twenty-three years later?

There is an active campaign to reverse anti-Trade Union legislation, spearheaded by the United Campaign To Repeal The Anti-Trade Union Laws: www.unitedcampaign.org.uk

According to them: "Most anti-Trade Union law was introduced by the conservatives between 1979 and 1995. These laws strengthened employers and weakened Workers. They undermined Trade Union constitutions, making them less effective. These laws must be repealed, not only because they are repressive, but also because they are illegal in themselves - they contravene the UK's international obligations under ILO Conventions, the Social Charter of the Council of Europe, and United Nations declarations and covenants.

"The Employment Relations Bill (based on the Fairness at Work White Paper) will still leave most anti-Trade Union laws in place. As Tony Blair wrote on 31st March 1997, the changes introduced in the Employment Relations Bill "would leave British law the most restrictive on Trade Unions in the western world." In particular, the Bill still does not give British Workers the right to Strike as in all other European countries.

"Positive legislation in the field of industrial relations is required - laws which will protect Trade Unions from legal attacks, allow them to operate democratically and protect their members; laws which restore and extend collective bargaining, give each Worker the right to Strike and be represented by a Union, protect Workers against exploitation, and provide the basis for a fairer and more just society."

In my opinion, only by fully repealing the anti-Trade Union laws and educating young people about their rights as Workers, will the full power of organised Labour re-emerge.

In the meantime the Trades Union Congress is still the largest voluntary organisation in Europe, with member Unions representing over six and a half million Working People. They campaign for a fair deal at Work and for social justice at home and abroad.

The impact of the influx of Workers from former Communist countries should not be underestimated. They come from a background of respect for Workers, and know historically about the power of Working People. Perhaps they will instil a pride in being a Worker, and remind their once-proud British colleagues that, as

Dolores Ibárruri, the great Spanish Communist, said: "It is better to die fighting than to live forever on your knees."

Or exhort them to:
>Rise like Lions after slumber
>In invanquishable number
>Shake your chains to earth like dew
>Which in sleep have fallen on you
>Ye are many
>They are few

These lines are from *The Masque of Anarchy* by Percy Bysshe Shelley, written to commemorate the Massacre of Peterloo on 16th August 1819 in St Peter's Fields, Manchester. Armed cavalry charged a peaceful crowd of around 60,000 people gathered to listen to anti-poverty and pro-democracy speakers. It is estimated that eighteen were killed, and over 700 seriously injured.

Peterloo was a critical event not only because of the number of people killed and injured, but because ultimately it changed public opinion to influence the extension of the right to vote and give us the democracy we enjoy today. (See www.peterloomassacre.org)

However, as already mentioned, since most of these Workers are economic migrants, they are here to earn a living. As one Estonian explained, they can earn four times as much here than they could in their own country. Many unscrupulous employers are employing them at a lower rate than British Workers and using this new source of Labour to drive down pay and further erode conditions for the existing Workforce. This is already leading to tensions which are more easily aimed at the unsuspecting Worker than at the boss.

## 22. The 1984 Miners' Strike
p.116 *Of course - Maggie's started on the Miners now.*
Corby people showed their support for the Miners in many ways. A Miners' Support Group supported by the Trades Council was particularly active. They held a stall every Saturday in the Market Square as well as door-to-door collections four nights a week. The donations of money, food and clothing were handed over to visiting Miners every month at the Labour Club, where the Support Group had an office base for eighteen months.

Local Hairdresser and Treasurer of the support group Alec McKinty recalled: "We collected a massive £22,000 during the Strike. Good-hearted folk would drop by to the shop and donate what they could from their Wages." The late Nellie Connaughty provided the collecting tins!

Corby Wimmin's Group attended the Miners' Wives Support Conference in Birmingham and made links with groups nationwide. This led to the organising of holidays in Corby for Miners' children.

When the conflict arose in the Nottinghamshire and Derbyshire Coalfields with the formation of the Union of Democratic Miners, Corby adopted one of the isolated Striking Pits, Langley Mill.

● Mr Kane presents the £135 cheque to Mr Connelly watched by Santa (Walter Lewin) and well wishers.

## TREAT FOR MINE KIDS

MINERS' children got a special Christmas treat when a group of Corby people travelled north to give them a party.

Santa Claus and a clown entertained 100 children at Langley Mill near Nottingham. Each youngster was given a tea and a present.

The trip was arranged by the Corby Miners' Support Group whose secretary, John Connelly, handed over £1,000 for the Nottinghamshire and Derby miners.

Before they left, group members were given a cheque for £135 from county council leader Jimmy Kane — £35 from the town's Labour party and a personal donation of £100.

Mrs Evelyn Reilly, organiser of the group's Christmas appeal, said: "I think it was a good morale booster for the parents and the children enjoyed the party.

The miners families think the people of Corby are doing a tremendous job.

"They all said it was a night they will never forget."

*Evening Telegraph*, December 1984

This article, clearly showing the support given by Corby people, was one of many pieces of memorabilia kept by Monty Monteith, a Steelworker who received a gift of a Miner's Lamp from grateful Miners for the hospitality he and his wife provided.

Sue Nathan, a Youth Worker at the time, also recalls receiving a Miner's Lamp as thanks for organising the Billy Bragg concert which took place on the last day of the Strike. Apparently he generously donated his fee! The Redskins had also appeared at the Festival Hall supported by local bands earlier on in the Strike.

Another memorable highlight by all accounts was Ann Scargill's speech at a particularly well-attended meeting at the Labour Club.

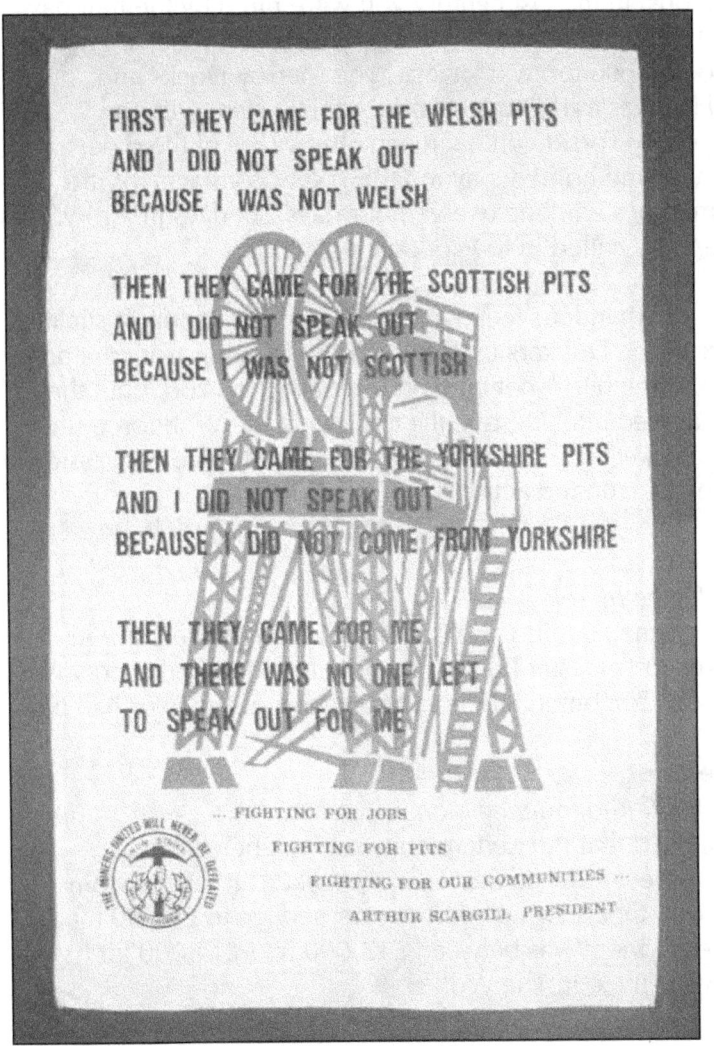

## 23. Dockers' history
p.119 *Back to the days of the Dockers*
Two generations have grown up with no - or very little - experience of the positive power of organised Labour.

As Annie explains in her monologue: "By the time they leave school the whole idea of a proper Job, a Job for life – Comrades, Workmates, common Trades and Skills to bind you together – will have gone. Call that progress? It's gone backwards – not forwards. Back to the days of the Dockers standing in pens on the Docks waiting to be picked for a day's Labour."

A Torside Docker explained: "Dock Work has always been associated with appalling working conditions. In the last century you were hired by the half-day from hiring pens with only a minority chosen for Work. Dockers received no pay if they weren't picked, so competition was savage. The Mersey Docks and Harbour Company (MDHC) was trying to reintroduce this system with the younger Dockers employed by Torside on nearly half the Wage of the older employees, with no sickness and holiday pay in 1995. New contracts for the older Dockers meant sometimes working twelve-hour days, six days in a row, and waiting by the telephone to be called in to Work on a day off.

"But the flipside to this is a tremendous feeling of solidarity, a tradition of sticking together against the boss. When Dockers used to be hired in gangs from the pens, they used their collective strength to "spot bargain" - refusing to Work until they were paid more than the agreed rate. Despite the decline in the Workforce since these days, rank and file Dockers still have a strong position to force concessions from the bosses when they take united action."

## 24. Which degree?
p.120 *I'd just finished a degree myself*
This image actually shows Irene Hamilton holding her Post-graduate Diploma in Management Studies, taken at Leicester Poly. The one referred to in the story was her first degree, a BA (Hons) Combined Studies from Nene College, Northampton.

## 25. Redundancy settlement
p.121 *My Johnny got £20,000 Redundancy Money*
John Wood-Cowling explained that the Redundancy settlement for the Steelworkers was the highest ever agreed for Manual Workers. It ranged from £25,000 for a First Hand Mill Operator with forty years' service to £6,000 for a new Worker. The average payment was between £12,000 and £14,000 for a Fitter who had been an Apprentice in The Works.

## 26. Immigration

p.126 *Imagine, British Workers ending up as immigrant Labour!*
After the Closure of The Steelworks, a significant number of unemployed people not only got on their bikes, but got on a boat or a plane and went abroad to look for Work. Two of the cast members were *Gast Arbeiders* (Foreign Workers) in Holland in the early 1980s "where Jobs were ten a penny".

It was a great equaliser to be "British Workers ending up as Immigrant Labour". I wonder how our experiences as economic migrants compared with those of the new arrivals from the Caribbean, pictured on p.126 arriving at Tilbury Docks in 1948 on Empire Windrush.

The "No Blacks, No dogs, No Irish" signs at boarding houses were not much of a welcome from the Motherland to those she had invited to fill the gap in Labour.

On a point of historical accuracy it is often erroneously believed that the Windrush generation were the first Black immigrants. In a recent play that Emma and I devised for Northamptonshire Black History Association, *River of Life*, we highlighted over 800 years of a Black presence here in this county.

## 27. Sit-in at Corby Clothing Company

Scene 4, p.136 *THIS FACTORY IS CONTROLLED BY THE...UNION*
This scene is entirely factual and this is a photo of the plaque which was awarded to Union Official Colin Tindley at the end of the dispute.

## 28. Routes for young people
Scene 5, p.140 *Enter* JEN, *another young woman*
In this scene the three young women follow very different pathways: travel, education and motherhood. We have included various helpline numbers on p.226 which refer to some of the issues raised, and also travel tips to encourage the reader to try the travel route.

## 29. Domestic abuse
p.141 *It was to a refuge in Wellingborough*
Corby has the highest rate of repeat-incidence domestic abuse in Northamptonshire, and for seven years had no refuge of its own. During the lifetime of this project CWTHG supported the campaign to get new refuge facilities for Corby, and have raised funds through performances of the play. We are pleased to report that just before Christmas 2007, new refuge facilities opened in Corby.

Domestic abuse is nothing new and is a muted theme threading throughout the book. From Gwenda discussing the neighbour's violent drunken episodes whilst Bridie remembers the nightmares of her own childhood in the 1934 *Homesick* scene, through the 1998 monologue where a young woman remembers having to escape to a refuge, to the Steel Kids' poem, "We take the knocks, the blows, the hammerings", violence in the home is an ever-present reality for far too many women and children. It ruins lives and every week two women escape the situation permanently - in a coffin.

When I returned to Corby from my studies and travels in 1983 I was horrified to discover the extent of domestic violence, and it was the spur which prompted the setting-up of Corby Women's Centre.

I remember vividly one incident soon after my return, when I was living with my sister Rebecca in the town centre. I answered an urgent knocking at the door at two o'clock one morning, to find a young woman covered in blood, wearing torn clothes and nothing on her feet. Her boyfriend had beaten her up in the back of the taxi on the way home after a night out, and then raped her before falling into a drunken sleep. That was when she managed to escape and had run across Corby to ask my sister for help.

This was my first face-to-face encounter with the ugly reality of domestic violence. We helped the woman as best we could. My sister patiently explained that this was not an isolated incident and described the abuse that went on in our street alone. I was shocked and horrified. Planet Paula had somehow avoided first-hand experience of domestic violence and I found it totally unacceptable. I still do. I wanted to write a book called *Did you hear the one about...* and simply tell these stories as a shock tactic. When I discovered what a lack of support there was for women, Rebecca and I decided to set up the Women's Centre, which to this day provides support for women involved in domestic violence, or domestic abuse as it is now called. The terminology was changed to acknowledge that the abuse is not only physical but may be emotional, mental and financial as well.

To live without fear is surely a reasonable expectation in a civilised society?

On International Women's Day, 8th March this year, some of us attended the Million Women Rise March in London - five of us, ranging from twenty-seven to fifty-one years old.

An international array of speakers spoke of female infanticide, honour killings, female genital mutilation, rape in war, trafficking, slave labour, and domestic abuse. Together we chanted the simple demand that violence against women must stop. It was heartening to see so many women joining voices to say "No, this is not acceptable!"

Hopefully this newly-invigorated wave of feminist activism, combining those of us who were there in the 1980s making similar demands with a newly-outraged and empowered generation of younger women, has the potential to achieve real progress in the eradication of violence against women.

It is time now to learn to treat one another with respect. Love that is tainted with fear is not love. In the meantime I applaud all those brave women who have endured, escaped and survived domestic abuse. "There is no excuse for his abuse."

There are safe spaces now, accessible via Women's Aid helpline (see below).

Although the large majority of domestic abuse is perpetrated by men against women, there is evidence of domestic abuse in same-sex relationships, and a growing number of men who find themselves the victims of abuse. There are helplines for both groups (see below).

Furthermore, this particular monologue was derived partly from a true story of a mother losing custody of her children to an abusive father who then went on to abuse the children. For any children in that situation helplines are also available.

| HELPLINE NUMBERS | |
|---|---|
| National Women's Aid | 0808 2000 247 |
| Broken Rainbow | 0845 2604 460 |
| Mankind | 0870 7944 124 |
| Childline | 0800 1111 |

## 30. Travel tips

p.145 *I'll do whatever it takes to keep me travelling*

Many young people in Corby, freed from the expectations of long-term loyalty to an employer, do the same as Jen did in her monologue. They Work long hours, save up enough money, and then go off travelling. The Women of Steel team includes three generations of travellers: Joyce, Lorraine, me, Rachel, Kenneth and Ali. Whether living in an Ashram, Working with abandoned children in Nepal, Walking to Moscow for World Peace, Fundraising for charity, or backpacking and Working your way around the globe, we have broadened our horizons through travel.

There are a host of travel opportunities waiting out there. Many countries have reciprocal VISA agreements with the UK, including Australia, New Zealand and most other Commonwealth countries.

Australia Working Holiday Visa
This visa is for people aged 18 to 30 years of age, who are interested in a Working Holiday of up to twelve months in Australia. This costs £90 British Pounds (GBP) or $190 AUD and you have to prove you have living expenses of $5,000 AUD (£2,260.53 GBP) in a UK bank account at the time of application. Most people borrow the money for a few days, get a printed bank statement, then apply for the visa. They then transfer the money back.

This visa allows you to supplement the cost of your holiday through short-term employment. If you are granted this visa you can:
- enter Australia within 12 months of the visa being granted
- stay up to 12 months (extendable to 24 months if you Work in Fruit Picking)
- leave and re-enter Australia any number of times while the visa is valid
- Work in Australia for up to 6 months with each employer
- study for up to 4 months

If you hold a second Working Holiday Visa, you may return to Work for a further six months for an employer with whom you Worked on your first Working Holiday visa. More information available at: www.immi.gov.au

Kenneth entered Australia on a one-year Working Holiday Visa. "I had £600 to my name when I landed in Oz and was lucky I had a place to stay on the Gold Coast with my good friend John Dunmore who was originally from Australia and had moved back out there. I had six interviews within two weeks and got a Job Working for the Red Cross Fundraising for charity."

"I got lots of little Jobs as I Worked my way around Australia. The employment was always of a temporary nature. This included Working as a Cocktail Barman at a resort (Magnetic Island); Digging Holes on a mango farm, always with a Spade at the ready in case of brown snakes! Planting rock melon seedlings (Bowen), Tele-marketing (Gold Coast), and Street Fundraising (Brisbane). All this paid some money, which I saved up to go camping for six months in tropical Northern Queensland, swinging from national park to national park in my tent. Lots of time spent out in nature. An inspirational time I shall never forget."

Kenneth continues: "I sometimes think you have to leave the UK to love it. These days, I would rather go to the Western Isles of Scotland than New Zealand."

Scenic Scotland

## 31. Pregnancy testing and teenage parenting
p.146 *I got pregnant not long after we got back*
In 1983 women in Corby started a free pregnancy testing service. Twenty-five years later, the service still survives, based now at Corby Women's Centre next to the library in Queens Square.

> **CORBY WOMEN'S CENTRE**
> **Free pregnancy testing and emotional support available:**
>
> Mon 9.30am - 12.30pm
> Tue, Wed, Fri 1pm - 4.30pm
> Thur 12 noon - 3pm
> Sat 12 noon – 2pm
>
> Tel. 01536 263156

Corby has had a high rate of teenage pregnancy for many years, at times topping regional statistics and attracting unwelcome media coverage. From my twenty years as a pregnancy tester, I concluded that for many young women with poor career options and only low-paid agency work on offer, there is no incentive to delay starting a family.

Corby has excellent support services for young mums: notably the Young Parents' Room and Chris Garvey, the Specialist Midwife for all teenage mums-to-be, based at the Pen Green Centre for the under-fives and their families.

For those young women who run into housing difficulties as a result of pregnancy, Corby has an excellent specialist facility.

> **EDEN PARK TEENAGE PARENT SUPPORT SERVICE**
>
> **Eden Park offers 13 one-bedroom flats and one two-bedroom flat for teenage parents aged 16-19, who are either homeless, or at risk of becoming homeless.**
>
> **Opened in 2006, it offers a safe, well-equipped and modern living environment, providing the chance to develop parenting and life skills with friendly and experienced staff on hand 24 hours a day to provide care for both mother and child.**
>
> **This includes support in pursuing educational and Job opportunities aimed at independent living. Facilities include a soft play area for children.**
>
> **If you would like to find out more about Eden Park or want to speak to the scheme manager please contact:**
>
> Eden Park, Elizabeth Street, Corby, Northants NN17 1SP   Tel. 01536 204315

## 32. Louise Allen

p.151 *after what happened to Louise Allen*
Louise Allen was tragically killed at the bottom of Sower Leys Road in Corby, trying to break up a fight between young women leaving the funfair. She was thirteen: one of the young people in Corby whose life has been cut short through senseless violence.

## 33. Statistics about Corby

p.151 *I mean, we feature at the top of all the statistics*
Things have improved in the ten years since 1998. However there is still a long way to go, as you can see from this snapshot of the town taken last year.

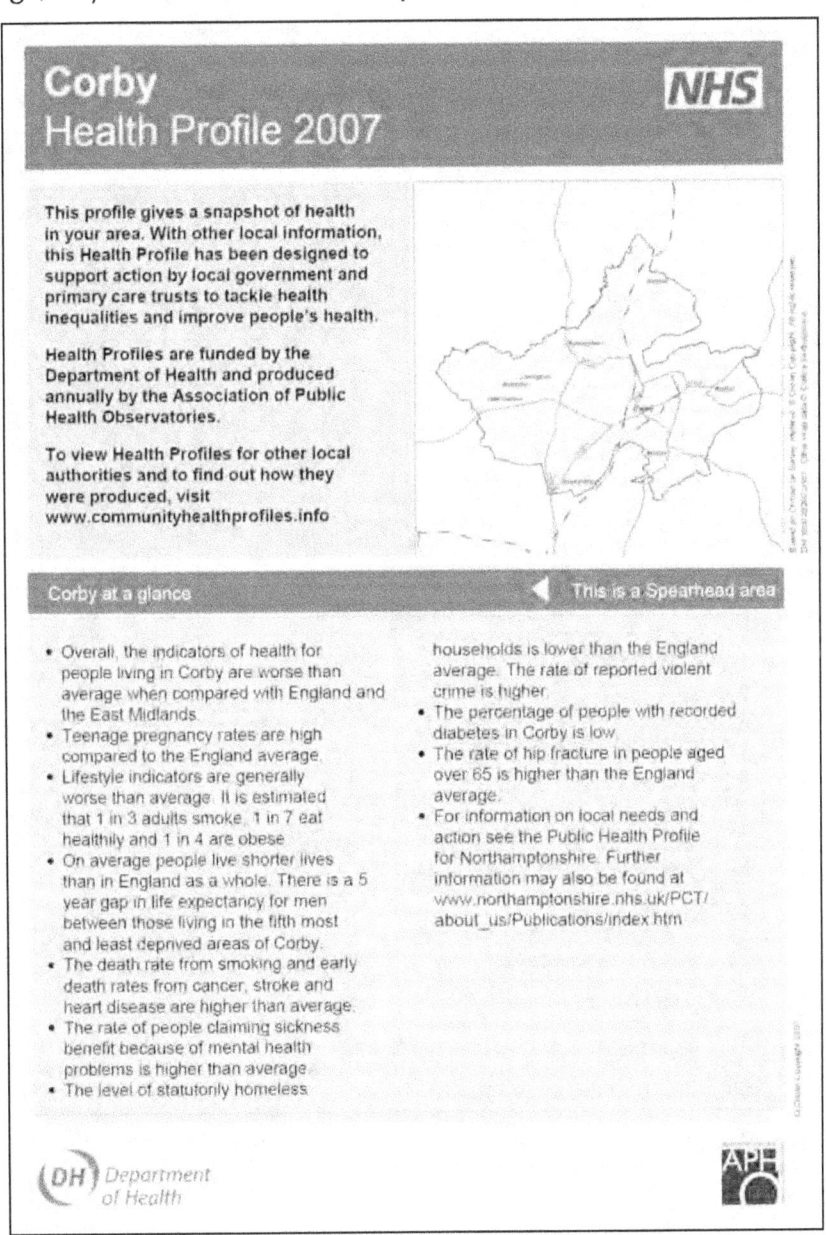

This chart shows a number of indicators of people's health in Corby.

| Domain | Indicator | Local No. Per Year | Local Value | Eng Avg | Eng Worst |
|---|---|---|---|---|---|
| Our communities | 1 Income deprivation | 7200 | 13.6 | 12.9 | 31.1 |
| | 2 Ecological footprint | n/a | 5.105 | 5.470 | 6.430 |
| | 3 Homelessness | 50 | 1.5 | 7.8 | 35.8 |
| | 4 Children in poverty | 2651 | 22.1 | 21.3 | 58.8 |
| | 5 GCSE achievement * | 469 | 60.1 | 57.5 | 33.6 |
| | 6 Violent crime | 1427 | 26.8 | 19.8 | 41.1 |
| Giving children and young people a healthy start | 7 Smoking in pregnancy | | | | |
| | 8 Breast feeding | | | | |
| | 9 Obese children | | | | |
| | 10 Physically active children * | | | | |
| | 11 Teenage pregnancy (under 18) * | 73 | 60.2 | 42.1 | 95.3 |
| The way we live | 12 Adults who smoke * | n/a | 34.2 | 26.0 | 37.3 |
| | 13 Binge drinking adults | n/a | 19.8 | 18.2 | 29.2 |
| | 14 Healthy eating adults | n/a | 14.3 | 23.8 | 11.4 |
| | 15 Physically active adults | n/a | 9.9 | 11.6 | 7.5 |
| | 16 Obese adults | n/a | 26.6 | 21.8 | 31.0 |
| How long we live and what we die of | 17 Life expectancy - male * | n/a | 74.5 | 76.9 | 72.5 |
| | 18 Life expectancy - female * | n/a | 79.8 | 81.1 | 78.1 |
| | 19 Deaths from smoking | 104 | 310.4 | 234.4 | 366.5 |
| | 20 Early deaths: heart disease & stroke * | 76 | 133.0 | 90.5 | 151.3 |
| | 21 Early deaths: cancer * | 85 | 153.7 | 119.0 | 168.0 |
| | 22 Infant deaths * | 3 | 4.2 | 5.1 | 9.9 |
| | 23 Road injuries and deaths | 38 | 70.8 | 59.9 | 214.1 |
| Health and ill health in our community | 24 Feeling 'in poor health' | 4869 | 8.7 | 7.8 | 15.4 |
| | 25 Mental health | 960 | 29.2 | 27.4 | 72.0 |
| | 26 Hospital stays due to alcohol | 121 | 222.2 | 247.7 | 652.4 |
| | 27 Drug misuse | 428 | 12.3 | 9.9 | 34.9 |
| | 28 People with diabetes | 1822 | 3.4 | 3.7 | 5.9 |
| | 29 Children's tooth decay | n/a | 1.6 | 1.5 | 3.2 |
| | 30 Sexually transmitted infections | | | | |
| | 31 Older people: hip fracture | 65 | 765.0 | 565.3 | 936.8 |

Heath Summary for Corby, Source: Department of Health Profile, 2007

## 34. The education route
p.152 *I knew my only route out of Corby was via university*

So what becomes of those who take the education route? To the town's loss, that is usually a one-way ticket. For years Corby has suffered a brain drain. But Corby is trying to remake itself as a place which will offer Graduate Employment. The first four Corby Zone Directors are all returned Arts Graduates. The company encourage others to return to Corby and they actively lobby to create opportunities for Arts graduates. This project alone has twelve graduates involved.

Big fish in a little pond

Many highly-educated young people have returned to the town wishing to be part of their community, and find themselves back down the agencies, saddled, as Emma says, with *"Debt! What a great start in life."* One interviewee told me that he Works at the Flour Mill with a nuclear physicist on one side and a maths graduate on the other. Neither have been able to find appropriate Work locally, but wish to live where they have friends and family. The daughter of one of the crew, a newly-graduated sociology student, is Packing shelves in ASDA and becoming ever more hopeless at the thought of finding Work here in her home town.

In many ways their frustration has parallels with the incoming communities. Rein Kubarsepp, an Estonian Film Director, now lives and Works in Corby. Amongst his friends are a former Czechoslovakian National Footballer and an Estonian National Opera Singer. The only employment they can find is as unskilled Labour. He Works full-time as a Carer.

It is imperative that there is a diversification of employment opportunities in the town if we want to reverse the brain drain and attract highly-qualified people to Corby.

p.152 *A little fish in a big pond*
Many talented young people leave, never to return. As Emma says, they are *"out there doing it, living their dream."*

And of course we could all name "Steel Kids" who have become "big fish in the big pond", and are making their way in the national and international arena.

## 35. Corby's reputation
Scene 6, p.154 *CORBY KEEP OUT!*
Corby has had a reputation for many years of being a "hard" town. With the demise of the Steel Industry and the resulting problems referred to in the *Wasted Years* section, this reputation grew steadily worse. In recent years this has become a problem for young people trying to make their way in a world where to admit to being from Corby can be a handicap. More recently, topping the statistics in everything from high fear of crime to teenage pregnancy has brought us a series of unwelcome articles from the national press, who seem to take a delight in building up stereotypically hysterical views.

This excerpt from the esteemed *Guardian* newspaper, no less, on 9th December 2006, gives a flavour of what has become all too common.

---

**BRITAIN'S OFFICIAL 'YOB CAPITAL' TURNS ITS BACK ON ASBOS**

With a metallic tinkle, a discarded can of Irn Bru is rolled by the wind along the pockmarked road outside the Arran community centre. Sheet metal is stapled over the windows of derelict flats nearby.

Corby in Northamptonshire has been branded the yob capital of an increasingly yobbish country...

One of the "most malformed places in Britain", according to *Country Life* editor-at-large Clive Aslet, Corby is also one of the largest towns in Europe without a railway station. Astonishingly, it has no cinema. And no bowling alley. It has the lowest proportion (8.5%) of working-age population with a degree-level qualification of any area in England and Wales...

If anywhere needed a good dose of Asbos, it would seem to be Corby.

The effect on the self-esteem of young people is clear to see. Many believe the reporting that the town is "the pits" and that means that they are too.

However, the fightback has begun, with such initiatives as the *Spirit of Corby* Awards and the *I Love Corby* campaign, which remind us all what is good about Corby. Mags McGuire, one of the staunchest defenders of Corby's reputation, traces her attitude back to her father:

"The older generation often have a fierce loyalty to the town. My Dad used to say: this town gave me a living and housed my family. If you don't like it, there is a bus leaves every day."

Whenever these articles appear, a whole range of people write in to complain. We do not take it lying down. Indeed two of the returned Graduates involved in *Women of Steel* answered a previous article by Clive Aslet who is mentioned in the *Guardian* excerpt above. Their comments are included here as evidence of the younger generation fighting for our reputation:

"I do not claim to understand the full extent of the development issues surrounding Corby. However I was born in Corby and have lived all my life here and I would admit we have our fair share of problems. However it is very sad and demoralising to read articles like this one that slate the reputation of the town. You have to remember that we are all living, breathing feeling people and these remarks are very cutting. I can honestly say I love living in the town of Corby because the community is great, and if this wasn't true and if every Corby person fitted into the stereotype we have received, then how is it that we have managed to run the country's only entirely voluntary theatre complex for over three years? Corby people do pull together and know there is more to life than money."
Jenny Garlick, 12th August 2006

"This kind of campaign is not what Corby or its people need! Anyone who has bothered to visit the town will find its inhabitants to be very friendly with a great sense of community. It has been very hard to live through the "wasted years" since the Steel Closures, and mistakes have indeed been made, but for the people in this town the hope of regeneration is great. We need to feel that we are worth a proper shopping area, leisure facilities and decent housing. I for one am doing all I can to aid the development of my town and change the public perception of Corby. Oh, and as for the green land comments: how much brown land are we supposed to have? Corby town wasn't built long enough ago to have enough brown land!

Stop kicking our town while it's down and do something useful instead, like backing the rail link campaign."
Emma Boulton Roe, 12th August 2006

## LOOK TO THE FUTURE

### 36. New schools for Corby

Scene 7, p.164 *schools which keep changing... the question is when?*
This scene was the dramatisation of an actual visit from the communications man from one of the major developers in Corby to Shout! Youth Theatre. He came bearing maps and talk of a shining future, only to be met with a deeply-ingrained cynicism, an expectation of more broken promises and some pretty straight talking.

I felt it was important to show how far things have moved on since the play was written in summer 2006, so I have included articles from the local *Evening Telegraph* newspaper which report on the progress of those promises. Here are two articles, the first about the rebuilding of Kingswood School, and the second about the new Academy. Plenty to be excited about for young people in secondary education.

# Blueprints for £26m school are revealed

■ By Kate Cronin

BLUEPRINTS for the £26m Kingswood School will finally go before planners tomorrow – and full details can be revealed for the first time today.

The designs feature a huge atrium covered in transparent material that will be used as a grand entrance hall.

As a specialist performing arts college, the plans are heavily weighted towards dance and drama, with facilities on the scale of a small theatre.

Pupils, along with the local community, will have access to tiered seating performance areas with professional sound and lighting equipment, a recording studio, five practice rooms and a sprung-floor, mirrored dance studio.

Outside is a Greek-style amphitheatre.

Facilities manager Sean Davison said: "We have arrived at these designs after consultation with the parents, students, staff and architects.

"We're looking forward to opening up this facility which will be fantastic for the children and the local community."

Sport is also well catered for, with a games area for four netball courts, eight tennis courts and a basketball court, fit all-weather pitches and football, hockey and rugby fields.

A sports hall with an electronic scoring system will be housed alongside a fitness suite with cardio-vascular equipment.

At the heart of the building are a cafe, deli and an open-air courtyard. A separate teaching space for sixth formers will be on the second floor.

The school will be built on a playing field between the existing Kingswood School and the former Our Lady and Pope John RC School in Gainsborough Road. Both schools will remain open during the building works but will then be demolished and replaced by homes.

School bosses are already in talks with Northampton College with regard to Kingswood providing BTec qualifications.

Birmingham-based architects Aedas say in their design statement: "The school could become a very central hub for lovers of the arts, sports and those wishing to further their education."

It is hoped the school will open to 1,200 pupils in 2010. It is being funded by £15m from the Government, £6m from the county council and the remainder from the sale of the land on which the current school stands.

The plans will go before Corby Council's development control committee tomorrow at Grosvenor House, George Street, at 7.30pm. The meeting is open to the public.

*Evening Telegraph,* Monday, 3rd December, 2007

# TOP ACADEMY TAKES SHAPE

## Ceremony to mark building of flagship school

■ By Kate Cronin

A FLAGSHIP £30 million school that will help revolutionise education in Northamptonshire is set to become one of the best in the country.

Dozens of civic dignitaries and project leaders have gathered for a traditional topping out ceremony to mark the completion of the roof at Corby Business Academy and celebrate the key landmark in the building of the school, which is set to open next September.

Corby MP Phil Hope told the guests: "This is going to be a fabulous building and one of the top academies in the UK."

The building will accommodate 1,250 pupils as part of the Government's flagship City Academy Scheme.

Pupils are expected to be drawn from a wider geographical area than other secondary schools in the town, with half of each year's admissions from Corby and the remainder from surrounding towns and villages.

The academy will replace Corby Community College, with current students at the college automatically transferring to the new academy. All new pupils will have to sit an entrance exam.

Construction of the school, designed by the world-renowned London-based architects Foster and Partners, at the site formerly earmarked for the failed WonderWorld project near Weldon, is already ahead of schedule.

Peter Simpson, chief executive of Brooke Weston City Technology College in Corby, will oversee the academy.

He said: "It will be an inclusive school providing the best possible education for every one of its students and, working in partnerships with the local business community. It will make a real contribution to the regeneration of the town that has now begun."

■ Continued on page 3

■ ON SCHEDULE – Corby MP Phil Hope tops out at the new academy, pictured above   *ET pictures by Alan Castle 140907-4-08*

*Evening Telegraph*, Saturday, 15th September, 2007

---

The school is being funded by the Government, the county council, Brooke Weston City Technology College, the Weston Foundation and Bee Bee Developments.

Corby Community College pupils Katie Harrison and Chris Usher wore the new green and black school uniform of the business academy as they helped out during yesterday's topping out ceremony.

Chris, a year 10 pupil, said: "It's very exciting. It will be nice to be able to have a new school to explore."

15th September 2007

### 37. Plans for new leisure facilities
Scene 8, p.168 *why haven't we got them now?*
In this scene young Kirsty reflects on the fact that her parents had a cinema, a bowling alley and buses that ran past 6.30pm. So in 2008, why don't we? How far have we got with providing the most basic of leisure facilities for the town?

Once more I have looked to the ET, which historically for many people is still the source of news about the town, as the headlines throughout the book show.

Interestingly enough, these two extracts, which appeared in the ET towards the end of 2007, seem speculative. However they show that a cinema, if not a cinema AND a bowling alley, are definitely on the agenda.

> **TOWN MAY BE SET FOR NEW CINEMA**
> CORBY could be getting its first cinema for years with talks under way to develop town centre offices. Corby Council is in talks with town centre owners Land Securities to turn Deene House in New Post Office Square into a cinema and multi-complex.
>
> EVOLUTION Corby – a huge £100m development – has been unveiled and is set to be another boost for the booming town.
> The scheme, including stores, homes, a community or sports centre and possibly a multi-screen cinema or bowling alley, follows the success of the new Willow Place shopping centre.

In the meantime, it is always possible to nip down "Rocky Hill" to Rockingham Village Hall to catch the touring Oundle Cinema on the last Friday of the month. What? You mean you didn't know about this well-kept secret? Me neither. But now I do, I intend to pass it on to as many people as I can.

So below are details of Oundle Cinema. Why not exploit our much-vaunted rural Northamptonshire location and enjoy exploring the quaint villages, real ale pubs and beautiful countryside amongst which we nestle – and follow it with a night at the cinema! Sounds much better than the X4 to Kettering and a trip to Burger King.

We are very good at DIY in Corby. So whilst the big developers and multi-million-pound cinema moguls deliberate over when the good folk of Corby can have a cinema, we have two solutions.

Corby Zone hope to be opening the doors of the Manor House on Cottingham Road as an Arts Space later this year. Although the building is mainly about space for creativity, with Artists' Studios and a Theatre Lab, there are some small performance spaces with independent film screenings planned for the very near future. There will also be a much-needed and long-awaited Art Gallery in the building.

And Oundle Cinema have agreed to do some screenings for us here in Corby. (See box for details of how to make a booking yourself.)

---

### OUNDLE CINEMA

Oundle Cinema is a community venture, run on a not-for-profit basis. Its main programmes are at the Stahl Theatre, Oundle, which it hires for the purpose from Oundle School. Full details of the current programme, including synopses and trailers, are shown on the Cinema's website: www.oundlecinema.org.uk

Outreach activity began in 2005. Support comprises:

- Discussing film selection and availability
- Booking the film with the requisite licence for public viewing
- Attending on the night with projector, screen, sound system and film
- Setting up, showing the film, packing up
- If required, we can also include a 'short' before the main film – a 5 to 15 minute film which is normally entertaining or challenging (can be selected to suit the audience and/or to complement the main feature). No extra charge!
- The minimum charge is £105 (essentially the cost of hiring / licensing the showing). We welcome a contribution to our overheads (say £25 - £50), if the revenue from the event is sufficient. The aim is for the village hall itself to make some money from the event, as well as covering the Cinema's costs.

The idea is that these events are primarily community events and should be marketed as such. Thus it is the responsibility of the organising body (e.g. Village Hall) to provide the venue (suitably licensed!), market the event, sell tickets, provide / sell refreshments, etc. Oundle Cinema really acts as an 'Intelligent Contractor', providing the screening service together with any advice needed.

Further benefits, funded through Rockingham Forest Trust:
- Multiple brochures to assist with marketing.
- Transport to and from film venues for those needing assistance.

### 38. More shops for Corby

*Scene 9, p.170* JEN *has just moved to Newcastle and is phoning her old friend* PHIL *back home in Corby*

In this scene a young woman who has just moved away from Corby to Newcastle phones a friend back home to tell him what a wonderful time she is having, with endless shops and leisure facilities. Her Corby friend's highlight is going to Home Bargains! This line got far too many laughs of recognition.

But that was July 2006. How far have we come in developing the town centre, and what does the next stage hold?

Land Securities, the company behind Willow Place, provided this outline of their next planned phase of development:

---

**EVOLUTION**

The new Willow Place shopping centre has transformed the retail heart of Corby. But this is only the first step in the town's renaissance. Land Securities has submitted ambitious proposals for a new phase of redevelopment which will firmly establish Corby as a thriving sub-regional centre.

We want to assist Corby to reach its full potential by creating a vibrant, mixed-use development in the heart of the town centre with retail, residential and community elements to meet the needs of present and future generations.

The scheme will include:
- A department store
- Up to 340,000 sq ft of new retail floorspace
- New apartments
- Two new car parks providing up to 1,600 spaces
- Improved routes and connections within the town centre
- Improved lighting, street furniture and signage
- Enhanced pedestrian and vehicular access, including improved waiting areas for public transport users
- Discrete service areas, with the majority of retail units serviced from underground to reduce vehicle movements in the town centre
- A community or sports facility
- The creation of a boulevard along Westcott Way

Drawing on our huge experience of retail development and management, our masterplan will set the benchmark in the region for good urban design, integrating seamlessly with the rest of the town centre. We intend to make the scheme as future-proof as possible and an exemplar of green urban redevelopment.

Our aim is to create a seamless piece of architecture in Corby that extends the Willow Place development, creating an attractive new urban quarter in the town based around a high quality public realm. Outdated perceptions of a once fragmented town will be left behind, to be replaced by a unified retail hub and a vibrant town centre.

However, I spoke to young people about how impressed they are with the new town centre, and the one thing they felt was missing was a music shop.

Fopp, the UK's largest independent music retailer, was due to take a shop in the new Willow Place, but went into liquidation before the move.

15-year-old Jack, who wrote this scene, said "I was gutted! I was well looking forward to it opening. I had my application form downloaded and everything, cos that's where I wanted to get a Saturday Job."

Hopefully an alternative is on the cards…

■ TOWN VISION – an artist's impressions of phase two of the regeneration of Corby town centre

*Evening Telegraph*, Wednesday, 12th March, 2008

## 39. Further education plans for Corby

Scene 10, p.175 LEE and JENNIFER, *two eighteen-year-olds, enter and sit down to discuss their future career options*

This scene looks at further education opportunities for eighteen-year-olds in Corby. The news on this front is good. Here follow two articles about future plans for Tresham College, including university college status. In the meantime, if the X4 could be replaced by a bus that went directly to Northampton and actually stopped somewhere useful when it got there, it would improve the likelihood of more Corby kids sticking with the courses already on offer in Northampton, without having to lose three to four hours travel time a day.

*Evening Telegraph*, Monday, 17th March, 2008

# £20m BOOST FOR COLLEGE

## Investment set to bring huge rise in student numbers

By Joni Ager

A MULTI-MILLION pound expansion at Tresham Institute is expected to see a huge rise in the number of students applying for courses.

The college, which teaches more than 2,300 full-time and 14,000 part-time students in the county, has revealed it will open its new £20.5 million building at Windmill Avenue in Kettering in April.

Tresham has also unveiled plans for a new state-of-the-art campus in Corby and has future plans for another new campus in Wellingborough by 2012. Senior Tresham staff are expecting their new facilities to contribute to a 20 per cent increase in people applying for courses over the next five years.

The new Windmill Avenue campus will include a performing arts centre, a new sports hall and a striking glass atrium.

Principal Stan Macdonald said: "It will be the best educational building in Northamptonshire."

It will be followed by plans for the redevelopment of campuses at Corby and Wellingborough, with more vocational courses to get people into skilled jobs such as construction and engineering.

Towns in north Northamptonshire have some of the lowest levels of post-16-year-olds with no qualifications in the South Midlands. In Kettering, eight per cent have no qualifications, Wellingborough 10 per cent, Corby 11 per cent and East Northamptonshire six per cent.

Corby MP Phil Hope, who is also the Government's skills minister, said: "Tresham has a crucial role to play in improving the skills of young people and adults in the workplace. Tresham is helping to achieve the social regeneration we need to match the physical regeneration of the area."

Pamela Hutchison, headteacher at Corby Community College, said: "Schools are encouraged to find the best courses and qualifications for youngsters between 14 and 19, whether that be in school, college or with work-based providers. The new campus will be great for Corby's young people."

Tresham is holding open days for prospective students at the Corby campus on Tuesday, February 6, in Wellingborough on Wednesday, February 7, and at Kettering on Thursday, February 8.

■ Special report – page 6
■ Work on £30m academy starts – page 3

■ THE FUTURE – an artist's impression of the Kettering campus, which is due to open in April

*Evening Telegraph*, Tuesday, 30th January, 2007

**40. Corby's future and the forces of global capitalism**
Scene 11, p.181 *Look to the future / Gleaming and bright*
What can we look forward to? This is what the Chief Executive of Corby Borough Council had to say about the future:

---

### DEEDS NOT WORDS

"Deeds not words is the Borough Council's official motto and it sums up everything we're about. No fancy promises we can't deliver. No gobbledygook about sustainable communities.

No glib, patronising statements about community involvement. Just a total commitment to improve our town and make it a great place to live, work and play.

We promised a new Town Centre and it's well on its way. We promised a new railway station and services are due to start in December. We promised to improve the older housing to make it as good as the new and we're already delivering on Kingswood with more to come in Arran Way and Danesholme. We promised to put Corby on the sporting and Olympic Map and we've done it with the new International Pool and improvements to Rockingham Triangle Stadium.

We promised to improve parks and green spaces and West Glebe carried off a national award as Best Community Project. But there's a lot more to come.

In the next three years we aim to attract a multiplex cinema operator, build new, dedicated youth and community buildings, and revamp East Carlton Country Park and more... much more!

We call it 'putting the Cor(e) back into Corby' and, believe us, there's a lot more to come!"

Chris Mallender
Chief Executive of Corby Borough Council

Our MP Phil Hope had this to say:

## CREATING A NEW CORBY

"The physical regeneration of Corby is there for us all to see as we walk around the town. But I remember as a founder member of 'Catalyst Corby' the doubts that people had: "It will never happen" or "I'll believe it when I see it".

Ten years on, we take these changes for granted. Corby has a new skyline. Some changes are here already – new town centre shops, new homes and new leisure facilities; some are being built today – new schools, new children's centres, a new swimming pool, a new theatre, a new library and a new rail station; and more are in the planning stage – an even better town centre and a new hospital.

But as well as this physical transformation, I detect a growing social change. I hear and see greater optimism and aspiration among Corby people than ever before. This kind of change is more profound and arguably more important than any other.

I hear young people at Corby schools talk about their desire to get better qualifications or skills to get a decent job. I see a return to full employment, and students who left Corby for university say how good it is to come back to their home town rather than have to live elsewhere.

I see a renaissance in the cultural life of Corby, with the new theatre, arts centre and library being built set to give a great boost to Corby artists. However I know that many people who are not in any way prejudiced feel uneasy at the arrival of the many new faces, cultures and languages that we see in Corby today.

But Corby's history is based on successive waves of people who migrated to the town for work – the Scots and the Irish in particular – and we have long had a strong local Polish presence. Although we have a relatively small Black and Asian community, we have many different cultures and communities in Corby, all of whom are living and working together very successfully. This diversity is widely recognised as one of Corby's great strengths.

At this year's Spirit of Corby awards I heard about the huge contribution that individuals of all ages, community groups and businesses are making to build a stronger community spirit in our town. This is the glue that binds together a Corby that is stronger because of its diversity and its many cultures.

I take great pleasure in hearing people talk about themselves, sharing my pride in our town and hearing their plans for a better future. Creating our 'New Corby' is the most exciting and exhilarating opportunity that I hope every person, whatever their age or background, is proud to be a part of."

Phil Hope MP

However, we must not forget that we are as subject to the forces of global capitalism as any other town. The endless pursuit of profit before people will continue to see whole Industries demolished, and Workers treated as an expendable and movable commodity. Brought down from Scotland to Work in The Works. Sent overseas in search of better pay and conditions. Invited here to fill a gap in the Labour market. Thrown on the scrapheap at the drop of a hat while your actual Job is exported to cheaper Labour overseas. Sound familiar?

It goes round in circles. But we know how to fight for our future here in Corby. We have done it before and we can do it again.

The following article is so reminiscent of the Fight to Save Steel that I wanted to include it. It has extra poignancy, as the reason given for the prison service moving out of Corby is that we are not ethnically diverse or highly-educated enough for them.

From a town where, according to council statistics, at least thirty-three languages are spoken, and where many of the town's Graduates come back to find no Graduate Employment and end up Working in Factories like everyone else, this is clearly an inaccurate representation of Corby, which prejudices views of the town.

■ TAKING ACTION – Crown House worker Marie Downie, backed by her colleagues, presents the petition to Corby Council chief executive Chris Mallender

# MP to hand over Job cuts petition

**By Kate Cronin**
kate.cronin@northantsnews.co.uk

A PETITION signed by more than 3,500 people will be presented to the Government in a bid to save 80 jobs in Corby.

Prison Service workers based at Crown House in Corby are fighting plans to move the jobs to Leicester before the Corby office block is demolished to make way for town centre regeneration.

Earlier this year, a leaked letter from Prison Service boss Ann Beasley revealed the service was being moved because Leicester had a more ethnically diverse population and more people educated to degree standard.

Yesterday, workers walked en masse to Corby Council offices to meet chief executive Chris Mallender for last-minute advice and to ensure council backing.

Corby MP Phil Hope was today due to hand over their 3,564-signature petition to prisons and offender management minister Maria Eagle MP.

Worker Marie Downie said: "People in Corby have been very supportive.

"At the moment the move to Leicester is still going ahead, but until we are actually sitting in that new building, anything can happen."

Corby Council and the North Northants Development Company have offered the Prison Service a range of old, new, refurbished and purpose-built properties to help keep the jobs in the town - but the Prison Service has failed to reply to any correspondence.

Mr Mallender said: "You would expect a public organisation to respond to requests and be open to dialogue.

"The Prison Service should be properly accountable but from our point of view this has been a bitter experience.

"We have fought the hard fight but unfortunately we have so far been unable to turn it around."

Mr Hope, who will travel to London today with Corby councillor Mark Pengelly to hand over the petition, said: "I want Maria Eagle to understand feelings are high among my constituents in Corby. I hope the Prison Service will reconsider."

A complaint was made to the Commission for Racial Equality as a move on such grounds could be racist.

The CRE promised to investigate the issue and Mrs Downie added: "We are expecting a reply very soon."

*Evening Telegraph*, Monday, 17th March, 2008

## 41. The Jobs market in Corby today

p.183 *SONG: GIVE US A JOB TO DO IN CORBY*

As with the opening of the Enterprise Zone, we became an area for investment in the 1980s. It is worrying to see this familiar-sounding headline twenty years on, but as I have already explained, it is yet more evidence of the circular nature of the capitalist economy.

# Job loss town set to get cash boost

**By Kate Cronin**
kate.cronin@northantsnews.co.uk

THE jobs market in Corby is set to be boosted by £2.2 million of European cash.

Corby Council, North Northants Development Company and Northamptonshire Enterprise Limited bid for the money from the European Regional Development Fund.

The town is the only one in the county to secure money from the fund, which is aimed at securing and stimulating enterprise and supporting the growth of new businesses.

East Midland Development Agency will hold the cash and decide what it can be spent on in the town.

It will be invested in Corby over the next three years and it is hoped it will increase levels of economic activity in the area.

One of the projects bidding for some of the money looks likely to be the Corby Enterprise Centre, which business leaders are hoping will be set up on the edge of the town to nurture small companies.

The news follows a spate of large-scale redundancies in the town - with Avon, Quebecor and Valassis laying off nearly 1,000 workers between them.

Chief executive of NNDC Bob Lane said: "This is a timely boost for the Corby economy and its workforce, which has felt the full effect of the UK's economic slowdown in recent weeks. Our job now is to use this funding to deliver maximum impact, both in terms of the number and quality of jobs created and ensuring residents have the skill levels and aspirations to fill them."

The programme of investment in Corby will focus specifically on projects and activities that promote economic growth by creating jobs and improving access to employment opportunities.

Its objectives include improving access to employment opportunities and reviving local infrastructure and environments.

Corby Council leader Pat Fawcett said: "Corby was one of the first areas to benefit from European funding in the 1980s. It had a huge impact on the economy and investment then, and although the sums are lower this time we are aiming to use them to equally positive effect."

Additional funding will be made available for activities that promote business creation and increased performance. As well as stimulating and supporting enterprise opportunities, the fund aims to increase access to finance, resources and business support for existing and new companies.

MP for Corby and East Northamptonshire Phil Hope said: "I am pleased Corby is to benefit from £2.2 million in European funding. It will go a long way towards promoting jobs skills and strengthen Corby's ability to flourish."

*Evening Telegraph*, Thursday, 12th July, 2007

## 42. Wages and conditions

p.183 *Pay us a living Wage in Corby*

In closing I would simply like to explore the final stanza of the song written in 1985 for *It Starts with the Ore* by Ian Cameron.

> *We've made this town our home*
> *Children and families*
> *Built it on hopes and dreams*
> *Built it on Iron Ore*
> *Give us a place to live*
> *Give us what is our due*
> *Just give us a Job to do*
> *In Corby*

At a time of high unemployment the battle was for Jobs. But these words could be expressing the sentiments of the economic migrants from Eastern Europe arriving in Corby with their Labour to sell and their families to feed.

For the 2006 performance, with high levels of people in Work, we decided to rewrite the last verse to reflect the high-employment, low Wage economy:

> *Now that we've come of age*
> *Give us what is our due*
> *Pay us a living Wage In Corby*

For some years now, Corby has had a high-employment, low Wage economy which destroys lives just as surely as no Work at all. Far too many young people find themselves still living at home because they cannot make ends meet on the national minimum wage and irregular employment offered at the employment agencies. Those who make it onto the housing ladder, either in private lets or council housing, soon find that it is impossible to make ends meet. Working your fingers to the bone to earn a pittance breeds poverty of spirit just as surely as the inactivity of unemployment did.

With unscrupulous employers now taking advantage of Workers arriving from Eastern Europe, often employing them for less than the indigenous population, there are fewer openings for young Corby people, and Wages and Conditions are being driven down.

And since the anti-Trade Union laws still remain on the statute books, to the shame of the Labour government, there is very little organised resistance.

It is not the bosses who bear the brunt of the inevitable hostility to those who are perceived to be "taking our Jobs".

As one cast member said to me before a rehearsal, in a broad Scottish accent: "Have you been up town lately? All they foreigners! You cannae understand a word they are saying!"

The circle goes round again. The same was said, though in a different accent, in the 1930s when the Tartan Army invaded a sleepy Northamptonshire village in search of a Job and a future.

The infrastructure of the town can be polished until it shines out like a beacon of hope, but without a massive improvement in the Wages and Conditions of the salt of the earth - the Men and Women of Steel who are the people of this town - that golden promise will never be enjoyed.

Paula Boulton
July 2008

# MISCELLANEOUS

## THE CREATIVE PROCESS

The process which led to the creation of *Women of Steel* as a site-specific promenade performance in 2006, and its adaptation to a stage play in 2007, is explained in the following report.

It was written in May 2007 for Corby Women's Theatre Group's AGM. All the people referred to are members of CWTHG - cast, crew or admin - and all are listed in the programmes.

In June 2007 we filmed the theatre version, and this is now available as a DVD with an accompanying CD of interviews not used in the play and music.

## CORBY WOMEN'S THEATRE GROUP
## DIRECTOR'S REPORT, MAY 2007

With the success of *Women of Steel* ringing in our ears, I thought I would take this opportunity to reflect on the process of its creation.

It is hard to believe that this time last year I was suffering from severe writer's block! Thanks especially to my script buddies Josie, Lorraine and Joyce, for supporting me then. I knew we had a first rehearsal booked, but after eighteen months of planning and raising the money, not a word had been written. The spark had gone out of the idea for me. At Christmas I had seriously considered giving up completely. But my nephew Jack gave me a pep talk and I promised him I would at least try.

One of the questions which occupied my thoughts as I was creating *Women of Steel* was: what was embryonic at the time of the Closures? What became of those new lives? How were they affected by the Closures?

Conveniently, my niece Emma was one such embryo. What an ideal opportunity to further our writing partnership! So we took a trip to Edale Youth Hostel, where we nailed down the creative idea, and I shared my thoughts with her about an outside promenade performance. We agreed that she should write the section about her era.

I was excited by the concept, but had no idea how to proceed. Normally I would have been stimulated by the interviewees. But now that the group had learnt to do interviews, they had done most of the Work themselves. And so it was that I started to listen to the interview tapes and acquaint myself with the Women of Steel being interviewed.

I had just heard Betty talking about her life to Joyce and found it thoroughly entertaining. I sat down at the computer and out poured the first three scenes: the house scene, the Blast-furnace, and the Cleaners' scene.

It has to be said that these scenes "arrived" from the ether. I could hear the voices from my childhood in my head with their rich variety of accents. Mrs Keenaghan and Mrs Jones talking to my mum about what they were missing. My mum's own heartache at having left her sisters, mum and the sea behind to come to Corby. Mrs Frazer who experienced the death of a loved one in the Molten Steel. I realised then that I knew the characters: what they would say, how they felt about life. I was simply giving them a voice and a presence.

I was very nervous as I turned up to the first rehearsal. I had asked for comments from my sister Julie, who would have recognised the stories, and my editor Val, in Wales, who wouldn't. And my script buddies mentioned above got a sneak preview.

The comments had all been positive. But this was finally it! I remember reading the scenes in all my different accents - and from that first moment, the group owned and recognised the characters. There was no "script critique" as such. The responses were about other similar women who they knew, or their own memories. And that was that! We were off.

The Women of Steel who are Corby Women's Theatre Group breathed life into the ghosts from the past who had come to me, and allowed them to live again. And I am sure I am not the only one to wonder when they will leave us be, as the project continues even now!

The process of finding the right accents was tricky. I knew that I needed an Irish voice for the house scene. I had had the pleasure of directing Bridie in 1991 in a play about AIDS. Rumour had it that she was due to move back to Corby. So I left her an answerphone message, and it was the first thing she heard on her arrival home! Luckily she agreed to join us.

With the cast assembled and the writing now flowing, it was time to get it off the page and onto its feet. We had a hilarious time at rehearsals - fuelled by Betty's snacks.

The women are a joy to direct, always supportive of one another and patient. The complexity of the piece would have challenged professionals. I never told them. I just used Paula's famous in-at-the-deep-end method!

The logistics were tricky and a constant shaper of the emerging play. "Should the scenes run clockwise or anti-clockwise?" isn't a normal consideration for a playwright or director. But given the layout of the building and the moving audience and scenes running concurrently, this was a key concern. Joyce's calm rational head was invaluable at these times. And of course, just when the group had got their heads round their part of the play, they had to redesign the concept to include Emma's section and the Shout! section.

Congratulations are in order to them all. To be still asking how many times they would have to repeat each scene the week before the performance indicates that this was never easy to grasp. It helped that we had the last few rehearsals at East Carlton Park to try to make it real. (The staff there were fantastically supportive.)

And quite apart from lines to be learned, the performers had meetings with Rebecca the costume mistress; there were tickets to be sold, transport to sort, media interviews to give, and photos to be taken! How ever did anyone find time for their other lives in the run-up to performance?

Behind the scenes there was a whole other script being created - the visual script. The stills script involved an informative training session for Lola and her assistants Lyn and Jan with Kevin Hayes, who had done the visual scripts for Banner Theatre when I toured with them in the 90s. Choosing from a myriad of images was a process in itself. These were then doctored by Lola, and the final stage was to involve Sami, our Video Editor, who also trained with Banner Theatre, in turning them into a usable format. I worked on the moving images with Sami, and her team included John from Professional Video Productions, and Andy Eathorne.

Then there was the soundtrack, which led to connections with all sorts of people, like Terry Sheen from the Male Voice Choir who sourced the Welsh music, and further liaisons with James Steventon who converted the records and CDs into digital format. Trips to East Carlton Park with Nick Maple, our technical manager, to plan the technical requirements, led to some funny moments. Once as I demonstrated the proposed Maggie Thatcher scene I was heckled by an innocent bystander, who turned out to be Jane Carr, the driver of the support vehicle on the Steel March.

The constant money battle bubbled away quietly. I got the council to agree to underwrite the marquee. Then argued with Corus and finally got £500 from them to fund it. Eventually we even raised donations for Corby Women's Refuge. And behind the scenes Irene balanced the books.

I convinced Stagecoach to provide transport for free, and one of the drivers, Estonian Film Director Rein, who I met whilst interviewing Bus Drivers about Corby, put us in touch with Sulev, a Russian Photographer, in the process.

Creatively, there were the parallel scripts being developed with Emma and Shout! and my decision to go for live music, which led to the re-arranging of songs and regular rehearsals with the wonderful Orebits. This was a band which had been put together for a play about Corby, called *It Starts With The Ore*, in 1985. There was also the challenge of involving ex-Steelmen, who had certainly had their differences at the time of the Strike.

And of course there was the building of the Corby Candle by Marian and Jenny, the unearthing of the ROSAC Banner from a dusty corner in the Festival Hall, and the procuring of the ISTC Banner which was loaned to us by Warwick University.

Eventually the three teams - Emma's gang, Shout! and CWTHG - met up with the crew and production team. Can anyone remember the huge circle at East Carlton Park?

The rest of the process is a series of snapshot memories for me:
- Recasting when we heard Lorraine's tragic news about her father the week before the show
- Joyce's news that we had sold out, which led to our decision to invite an audience to our dress / technical rehearsal
- Being filmed
- Having to perform as Karen in Lorraine's place
- Seeing the Marquee for the first time
- Sue, John and Adam building the stage
- The rain… and trying to decide during Act One whether to hold the Demonstration indoors or outdoors
- The first aid crisis when a Shout! member passed out
- The firework exploding one night and NOT the next because that dog walked past as it was about to be lit!

- The WonderWorld calypso procession
- Competing with the outdoor karaoke right next to the Marquee - especially when they sang *Stand by your man* while Jen described her mum escaping from domestic abuse
- Sending in Jim McDonald to try and negotiate with the party throwers
- The huge audience
- Sleeping in the Marquee as security
- Great feedback
- The after-show party

Three things I do clearly remember:
- The absolute dedication and mutual support between the Women of Steel
- Their brilliant, moving performances
- Everyone being in the right place at the right time

Did we ever expect it to be such a success?

CWTHG can be justly proud of having been part of a truly unique event and having done something to give Corby back some self-esteem.

Then, one month after the show, I saw what Sami and John had initially made of the filming, and we spent hours doing the best we could to turn a three-dimensional experience into a DVD.

The film night was a great time for us all to meet up again. Despite all our reservations about the DVD, it was advertised on *the best of Corby* website as a film that newcomers to Corby should see, as it "gives the viewer a greater understanding of Corby's make-up and what makes this town so special".

Then came the social evening at Margaret's, where the women's belief in the play as an important social message began to wear down my "never again" attitude. So I committed to finding a way for us to re-do the play on International Women's Day.

Working with Marian Anderson from Corby Zone, we successfully submitted a bid to Awards for All with the support of FORTAC for the Stories of Steel project:
- To rewrite the play for theatre performance
- To film it
- To produce an annotated script book
- To create a sound montage of new interviews
- A launch with a photo archive of the process

This led to *Women of Steel* Mark II. Suffice it to say that the re-writing was a joy. Once I had the concept of the table as the object around which everything would revolve, serving to shift the action from the domestic sphere of hearth and home onto the Workplace and then onto campaigning, I was enthused afresh. And it's a different process deciding what to chop rather than what to add.

My memory of the re-grouped Women of Steel rehearsing is watching them realise how easy it is to perform a play when it's done from start to finish in one space!

Given that for some of them *Women of Steel* Mark I had been their first-ever performance, it had defined their expectation of what being involved in a play would be like.

Their adaptability was remarkable. Just as well, because Lola was only able to commit to playing Isa, Danni was unavailable, and sadly, Josie fell ill and had to drop out of rehearsals.

Re-casting involved some interesting and memorable solutions:
- Bringing in Kim McGowan to heckle the character of her own mother!
- Emma playing Jean and also playing her younger self
- Playing Maggie Thatcher, with Rebecca on standby when I lost my voice
- Joy Elizabeth doing Maureen's story and Josie's monologue
- Jo playing the new character which replaced Danni's story
- Julie as narrator

Emma and I had rewritten one of her monologues and the demo scene was scripted. Shout! were hard at it, polishing up their contribution. The visual script had needed re-adapted to match the new play. This time it was done by Sami, Andy and me.

What fun realising the 1812 Overture version of the demolition! I had shared the idea with the Shout! young writers at their residential weekend and Claire and Leanne had cobbled some images together with the soundtrack. Lyn had coincidentally been experimenting with "wobble" on her images, and Sami and Andy finally sorted the spectacular final version.

One of the trademarks of CWTHG is the willing involvement of a whole chain of people in our process. Again, behind the scenes, production team, technical crew and front of house were all hard at work. This time things were easier for me, as Marian was project manager.

The sell-out of tickets surpassed our expectations again. We had hoped to sell 150 a night. To have sold 180 per night was testimony to the play's popularity. It also allowed us to raise another donation for the refuge.

Preparations were also underway for the filming day when sadly, due to illness, Rachel the film-maker dropped out. Nevertheless, we had two spectacular performances in the beautiful Arc Theatre, to very enthusiastic full houses, photographed by Kenneth and Rein and videoed by Joy.

The founder of ROSAC was in the audience and we had a letter of endorsement from Phil Hope, our MP. Some folk were there for a second time; others had not been able to get a ticket in the summer. They laughed and cried with us, as once again we told the story of Corby!

Curious about our roots as a theatre group, I watched the DVD of our last play *Our Bodies Ourselves* recently. I was thoroughly moved and entertained.
I realised then that our formula is:
- We do not shy away from painful truths
- We can laugh at ourselves
- We tell it like it is

And in doing so we have created a truly accessible style of theatre. Here's to our continued success as a group.

Paula Boulton
Proud Director of the one and only Corby Women's Theatre Group!


## AFTERWORD

In the interests of completeness, I wanted to describe the creative journey that took us from play to book.

At the end of CWTHG's 2005 production *Our Bodies Ourselves,* Lyn Plumpton, our Videographer, made a fancy cover for the script, and we gave the cast a presentation copy and a DVD of the performance.

Following the filming of *Women of Steel* in July 2007, we had the same idea, except that this production also included images and songs.

So we came up with the idea of an annotated script, purely as a memento, with the slides printed on the page next to the text over which they had been projected.

Lyn did a mock-up of the first scene, and from a quick pass-round it seemed we had general "thumbs up". But we very quickly hit a snag - the quality of images. What had worked, projected on a big screen for a few fleeting moments, didn't stand up to close scrutiny on the printed page. Also, as part of Corby Zone's emphasis on training, mentoring and skill-sharing, we quickly realised that there were skills we needed to learn if we wanted to make this more than a loose-leaf script with photos.

That's when Marian Anderson from Corby Zone told us that Kenneth Martin, who we knew as a Photographer on the project, had the necessary skills, knowledge and experience of layout and publishing to help us.

His vision for the project was immediately bigger. Firstly, he suggested that this could be the first of a series of community publications, and so we registered Corby Zone as a publisher with our own ISBN numbers. Secondly, he realised that there would be a wider market for such a publication - not just the fifty-odd cast and crew who had been involved in the film and play, requiring a humble print run of one hundred. The numerous local history books have a great following, and he could see that this would have a place next to them on the bookshelf.

So I both blame and thank Kenneth! What might have been a simple pamphlet has blossomed into this wonderful creation. A book, a proper book, with a print run of 1,000 and an expanded budget to match.

From Kenneth I learned the phrase "to scope a project". And I can assure you that this project had been seriously underscoped!

Jan Timmins and Lyn Plumpton amalgamated our initial selection of images. Then it was over to Kenneth to source the originals with the help of Lorraine Dziarkowska and Dr Peter Hill. At this point we entered the intricate and "finickity" maze that is Desktop Publishing.

And many months later, here we are. You are reading the result!

We hope that the lessons we learned during this process will be applied to future community publications, which can now, thanks to Kenneth, be published by Corby Zone.

As to the future: I look forward to encouraging others through the publishing process, in order to get their words in print.

In closing, I know that there are many talented writers in this town and many more *Stories of Steel*.

One ex-Steelworker, Willy Barr, sadly died of lung cancer the day I went to record him for this project. With him died a whole oral history. There is work to be done, more Stories to collect, so let's get on with it, before it is too late!

Paula Boulton
4th April 2008

# CAST LIST

If two or three performers' names appear, the first one played the character at East Carlton Park, the second (*in italics*) at the Arc Theatre and the third (underlined) in the film.

| | |
|---|---|
| NARRATOR | Paula Boulton / <u>Julie Steventon</u> |
| IRENE | Irene Hamilton |
| | |
| GWENDA | Margaret Marshall |
| BRIDIE | Bridie Norton |
| ISA | Lorraine Dziarkowska |
| MAUREEN | Josie Cassidy / <u>Joy Elizabeth Surgey</u> |

Cleaners in the Quantivac, 1960:

| | |
|---|---|
| CISSIE | Bridie Norton |
| ELSIE | Betty MacPherson |
| MARY | Irene Hamilton |
| MEGAN | Margaret Marshall |
| SALLY | Danielle Boulton/<u>Lorraine Scatterty</u> |
| MAVIS | Josie Cassidy / *Julie Steventon* / <u>Joy Elizabeth Surgey</u> |
| | |
| LORRAINE | Jo Alderson |

Canteen Workers, 1979:

| | |
|---|---|
| ELAINE | Betty MacPherson |
| ANNIE | Bridie Norton |
| RUBY | Betty Brown / <u>Karen McGowan</u> |
| JEAN | Emma Boulton Roe |
| YVONNE | Margaret Marshall |
| ISOBEL | Irene Hamilton |
| | |
| KAREN | Paula Boulton / <u>Lorraine Scatterty</u> |
| MAUREEN JOHNSON | Josie Cassidy/*Emma Boulton Roe*/ <u>Joy Elizabeth Surgey</u> |

Steelworkers from the Save Our Steel March:

| | |
|---|---|
| PETER | Peter McGowan |
| MONTY | Monty Monteith |
| STEELMEN | John Cowling, John Forshaw, Jim McDonald/ Kenny Bell, <u>Geoff Hirtsch</u> |
| CROWD | Shout! Youth Theatre <u>and the cast</u> |
| | |
| MAGGIE THATCHER | Josie Cassidy / *Paula Boulton* |
| BODYGUARDS 1 & 2 | Lee Docherty; John Connelly / <u>Phil Jennings</u> |

PIED PIPER OF WONDERWORLD        Joris Alexander

Box Factory Workers, 1984:
| | |
|---|---|
| JAN | Jo Alderson |
| KAREN | Lorraine Scatterty |
| JEAN | Lorraine Dziarkowska / _Emma Boulton Roe_ |
| ANNIE | Bridie Norton |
| JOSIE | Josie Cassidy / _Joy Elizabeth Surgey_ |
| ELAINE | Betty MacPherson |
| YVONNE | Margaret Marshall |
| ISOBEL | Irene Hamilton |

Workers at Corby Clothing Company, 1984:
| | |
|---|---|
| SUSAN | Emma Boulton Roe |
| MARGARET | Margaret Marshall |
| BETTY | Betty MacPherson |
| LIZZIE | Bridie Norton |
| JOY | Josie Cassidy / _Joy Elizabeth Surgey_ |
| IRENE | Irene Hamilton |
| EVELYN | Jo Alderson |
| | |
| SUPERVISOR | Crystal Dziarkowska / _Kim McGowan_ |
| ELLEN | Betty Brown / _Lorraine Scatterty_ |

Workers at a Chocolate Factory, 1998:
| | |
|---|---|
| DANNI / JO | Danielle Boulton / _Jo Alderson_ |
| EMMA | Emma Boulton Roe |
| JEN | Jennifer Ross / _Alison Hannah_ |

STEEL KIDS        Shout! Youth Theatre:

Joris Alexander          Jodie Mallett*
Georgia Britton          Kirsty O'Neil
Robert Cain              Amy Pointer*
John Connelly*           Jennifer Pyper
Lee Docherty             Jack Boulton Roe
Tony Giles               Danielle Skillen
Kirsty Graham            Leanne Villette
Philip Jennings          Shareace White
Terri Langley

* perfomed at East Carlton Park only

YOUNG NARRATOR        Leanne Villette

The following characters appeared in the East Carlton Park version only:

| | |
|---|---|
| DEVELOPER | Mark Conway |
| KIRSTY | Kirsty Graham |
| PHIL | Philip Jennings |
| JEN | Jennifer Pyper and Leanne Villette |
| PHIL'S INNER VOICE | Jack Boulton Roe |
| JEN'S INNER VOICE | Tony Giles |
| LEE | Lee Docherty |
| JENNIFER | Jennifer Ross |
| JODIE | Jodie Mallett |
| JORIS | Joris Alexander |
| MODELS | Terri Langley, Georgia Britton, Shareace White |

## COMMENTS FROM CAST MEMBERS

"I felt it was imperative that the story of Corby's history was told and it was a privilege to take part in this play. Hopefully people will recognise the same need families had to uproot from their homes and familiarity as the new migrants are doing now. My parents missed Scotland every day they have been in Corby but put their heart and soul into making this town a decent place to live. To understand the history is to know the people of Corby who made the town one to be proud of.

"My thanks to Paula Boulton for allowing me to take part and for recognising the need to tell the story and did so, brilliantly."

Lorraine Scatterty

"Participating in the play was very emotional for me. For the first time in 25 years while watching the audience reaction, as we acted, I realised that my family was part of a group of a very much larger family of Corby people. We had all suffered together, now we were telling their story as well as our own. True dramatic stories, which would make a truly great film."

Irene Hamilton
(Proud to be called Narrator in the book)

"I found it a great privilege and an unforgettable experience to have been involved in Corby Women's Theatre Group's production of *Women of Steel*. It gave me a greater insight into that particular era of Corby's history and a renewed sense of pride in the town and its people.

"The drama portrayed a time of flux and change in Corby's evolution. It traced the rise and the demise of Steelmaking as the town's foremost Industry, exploring too, real-life stories of those who came here to work and live and who struggled and fought through that time of crisis.

"Working within the group was a joy. We knew that our Work was an important record of those people and that time, and, despite a rigorous rehearsal schedule, we threw ourselves into the demands made upon us so that the story could be told.

"Audience response following each performance, demonstrated the extent to which hearts and minds had been moved and uplifted. Many had lived through the events; others understood, perhaps for the first time, something of their heritage. Thanks to the rest of the cast, and to our Director, Paula Boulton, who gave us the confidence to achieve this wonderful and valuable piece of Community Theatre."

Josie Cassidy, March 2008.

"The thing I miss most since the Steelworks closed is the Corby Candle. When I went on holiday or a trip to Skegness for the day, as soon as I arrived near The Works and saw the blazing Candle, I would get a nice warm feeling that I was home.

"I also have some great memories from when I was a Cleaner in The Works. I met some great characters and heard some hilarious stories from the other Cleaners. We had many a laugh. Oh well! In days gone by."

Betty MacPherson

## About the Play - Content

The play has been created and performed to look at where we are 25 years since the Steel Work closure, honour the struggle to Save Steel and acknowlege the fact that hard working people have come to Corby from all over the world for 70 years. Sharing our rich history with the new Corby people will show them they can be proud of the town they have chosen to live in, and join us in looking to a great future.

## About the Play-Style

The play is a unique, multi-media, site specific event where the audience move around live exhibits in the heritage centre. Drama, visual image, voice montage and live music are interwoven to tell the true stories of the Women of Steel and the Ore Kids who lived through these turbulent times.

## Performers and people

Corby Women's Theatre group formed in September 2004 to do this play. Originally the group was funded as an evening class by the Workers Educational Association, which enabled Paula to share the entire process of " Creating a community Drama". Over 25 women have been part of the group at some stage, and all have contributed their life experience to the process.

Shout! Youth Theatre was formed in 1998 by Paula and Emma. All 4 younger women are former members of Shout!. The group regularly create unique pieces of theatre as commissioned. Earlier this year they toured Northamptonshire libraries with their play about teenage pregnancy "To Do Or Not to Do" If you are interested in joining either group contact Paula on 01536 741922

Our guest performers are all former steel workers who walked to London with the Save Steel petition.

We are proud to welcome Emma Boulton Roe to the project. Born in 1980, Emma is a newly returned Performing Arts graduate and she wrote the section of the play which looks at how it was to grow up in Corby since Steel.

# Performers

## Shout! Youth Theatre

Joris Alexander
Georgia Britton
Robert Cain
John Connelly
Lee Docherty
Tony Giles
Kirsty Graham
Philip Jennings
Terri Langley
Jodie Mallett
Kirsty O'Neil
Amy Pointer
Jennifer Pyper
Jack Boulton Roe
Danielle Skillen
Leanne Villette
Shareace White

## Corby Women's Theatre Group

Jo Alderson
Danielle Boulton
Betty Brown
Josie Cassidy
Lorraine Dziarkowska
Irene Hamilton
Betty MacPherson
Margaret Marshall
Bridie Norton
Emma Boulton Roe
Jennifer Ross
Lorraine Scatterty

*With guest appearances from:*
*Mark Conway and*
*Crystal Dziarkowska*

Steel Men:    John Cowling
                Jim McDonald
                Peter McGowan
                John Forshaw

## The Orc Bits

| | |
|---|---|
| Paula Boulton | Violin and vocals |
| Ian Cameron | Vocals |
| Alan Hewitt | Whistle, percussion and vocals |
| Benita Hewitt | Accordion and Flute |
| Clive Parker | Banjo and percussion |
| George Reilly | Guitar and vocals |
| Emma Boulton Roe | Guitar and vocals |
| Rebecca Boulton Roe | Vocals |
| With Jack Boulton Roe | Drum |

# Act One

The play unfolds in many locations. Please stay with your groups and your stewards will guide you. The scenes can be viewed in any order.

### Café
**Roots**

---

### Works
- Jobs May Come 🎵
- Reservoir Song 🎵
- Morgan Squire 🎵
- In the Shadow of the Works 2000
  by *Emma Boulton Roe*
- My Home 2000
  by *Emma Boulton Roe*

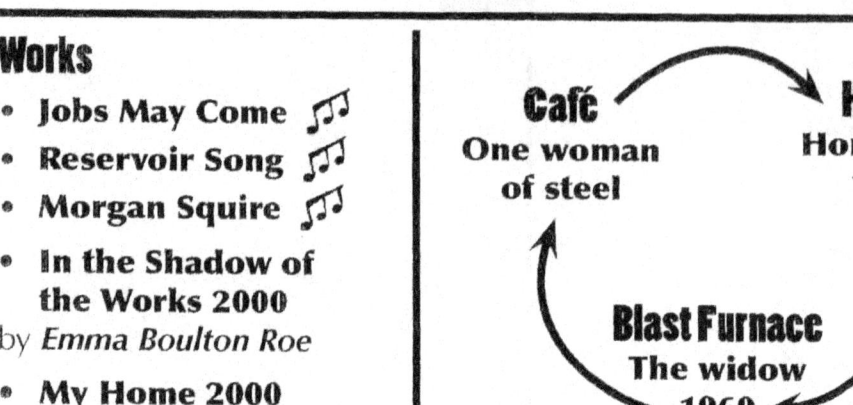

Café — One woman of steel
House — Home-sick 1934
Blast Furnace — The widow 1960

---

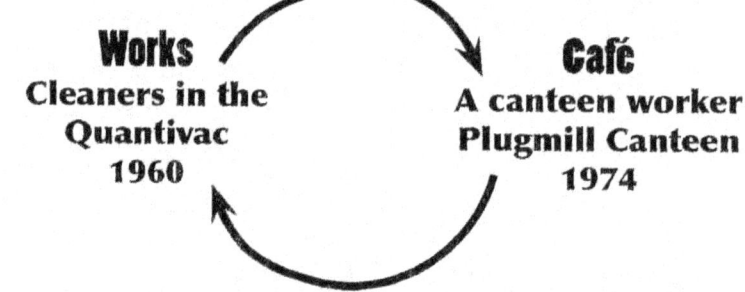

Works — Cleaners in the Quantivac 1960
Café — A canteen worker Plugmill Canteen 1974

---

### Café
- As the work grows, so the town goes 🎵
- Canteen 1979 Union meeting

---

### Patio
- R.O.S.A.C. demonstration
- The end of steel

# Act Two

## Outside
### Wonder World Calypso 🎵

*Please follow the Pied Piper of Wonderworld to the marquee*

## Marquee

Era  *Wonderworld Wonderwhen? 1984*
- **Broken Dreams**
- **The Aftermath**
- **Stand Your Ground**
- **Goodbye to Wonderworld 1990**

Era  *Wasted Years 1990 - 2005*
- **Asbury's Chocolate Factory 1998**
  *by Emma Boulton Roe*

Era  *The Present Day* ➡
- **Steel Kids**
- **The Future**
- **Our Reality**
- **I wish**
  *by Kirsty Graham*
- **Til the end**
  *by Jack Boulton Roe and Tony Giles*
- **A cut above**
  *by the performers*
- **Hope for the future**
- **Give us a chance** 🎵

## The End

## Music

| | |
|---|---|
| *Village Life* | Orebits |
| *Keep the Candle Burning* | Mike Carver |
| *Happy Town of Steel* (words and music) | Bobby Civil |
| *Sweatshop* and *Broken Dreams* | Banner Theatre |
| *Wonderworld* | Ian Cameron |
| *Old Corby Song* | handed down by Mary King to her daughter Ann Brown |

All other songs written and composed by the OREBITS for **It Starts With the Ore** in 1985.

N.B. All of the songs tonight are available on CD. Contact Emma tel: 01536 262054

## Creative Team

| | |
|---|---|
| Costume Mistress | Rebecca Boulton Roe |
| Set Design & construction | Marian Anderson with Jenny Garlick |
| Poster design | Lyn Plumpton, Jan Timmins |
| Programme design | Corby Community Arts |
| Dialect coach | Maggie Marshall |
| Visual Script | Lorraine Dziarkowska community photographer. |
| Assistants | Lyn Plumpton, JanTimmins With James Steventon & Marian Anderson |

Access to the ET library has been invaluable. Liz McBride, thanks for her co-operation. East Carlton Park for providing copies of their archive material. Kevin Hayes for training. The images have been researched from a wide variety of places and many from my own collection, a real community spirit, many thanks to all who contributed. Apologies to those who have not been acknowledged personally.

## Technical Crew

| | |
|---|---|
| Technical Manager | Nick Maple |
| Technical assistants | Andrew Maple and Mat Newman |
| Video editing | Sami Scott with Professional Video Productions and Andy Eathorne |
| Sound editing & projection | Sami Scott |
| Film Crew | Ellie Morton and Professional Video productions |

## Venue & stage management
Joyce Stirling

## Administration
Jo Alderson, Lorraine Scatterty, Lyn Plumpton

## Front of house team
Joyce Stirling with Daisy Dziarkowska

## Research
Thanks to John Wood Cowling, Jim McDonald, Peter McGowan, John Forshaw, Frank Smythe, Mick McGowan, Aidan Coleman, Jane Carr, Peter Floody, Norman Coates.

## Interviewees
Jean Hall, Winnie Scott, Anne-Marie Lawson, Maureen Forshaw, Betty MacPherson, Lorraine Dziarkowska, Joyce Stirling, Carol Lowe, Stanley Boulton, Eda Wood, Shirley White, Rachel Arnold, Sami Scott, the cast and past members of CWTHG.

## How it happened
"I finally got the funding for the bulk of this project in Dec 2005, 18 months after I started! I was ready to give up at that point. The anniversary year had come and gone and my enthusiasm was waning! Until a walk in East Carlton Park and the memory of a wonderful outdoor event collided and I was off again with the idea of writing the play around the heritage centre! Thanks to Jack, Sue and Emma who pushed me to do it, and the women of steel who have stuck with it throughout. I believe between us all we have created something unique which has taken on a life of its own."

*Paula Boulton*

## Thanks

This whole project has been a great team effort. Many people have contributed time and energy to make it a reality. Too many to list. But especial thanks to Pete Rob, Aidan Coleman and the staff of East Carlton Park, Peter Floody, our Stewards, The Lighthouse, Rotraut Anderson, Bob Chapman for sharing the vision, Madelyn McAlpine, CBC print room, Pete Weston, Ruth Tindley, Rockingham Primary School for stage blocks, Ken Penton from Community trade union for the loan of the ISTC banner, Eammon Norton, Corby Trades and Labour club for rehearsal venue, Julie Steventon and Val Stein for script critique and editing, our bus drivers Rein, Lisa and Alan.

## Corby Women's Refuge

Any proceeds from the performances will go to the new Corby Women's Refuge. Corby, the town with the highest rate of Domestic Violence in the county has been without a refuge since 2000. Several of CWTHG are involved in establishing a new one. This is our chosen charity. The new refuge is now in planning stage and will hopefully be open within a year.

## Men of Steel

Paula's next project looks at the men's experience of the Steel works. If you wish to contribute, please contact Paula on 01536 741922.

## Sponsors

An anonymous donor who believes in the future of Corby
Corus
Stagecoach

**Funded by**

## ADDITIONAL SONG LYRICS

OLD CORBY SONG

DRINKING SONG

RESERVOIR SONG

ACCIDENTS

AS THE WORKS GROWS

HAPPY TOWN OF STEEL

The *Orebits* were reconvened for the 2006 production of *Women of Steel*, having originally formed in 1985 for the Corby Community Arts production *It Starts With the Ore*. They were joined by Emma and Jack Boulton Roe.

# OLD CORBY SONG
## Handed down by Mary King to her daughter Ann Brown

Life was hard for the new arrivals in the 1930s, and some people made a lot of money from immigration, like Morgan Squire's, the furniture store in the old village.

*I took a trip to Corby*
*Sure they said 'twas paradise*
*But when I reached the station*
*Sure the tears fell from my eyes*

*There were English, Welsh and Irish*
*There were Germans there as well*
*But as for us poor Scots folk*
*Sure we might have been in hell*

*So goodbye dear old Corby*
*From you I must depart*
*For if I do not leave you*
*You will break my bloomin' heart*

*And if you ever go there*
*And if you should enquire*
*Of the man who made the money*
*'Twas an old git called Morgan Squire*

*So goodbye dear old Corby*
*From you I must depart*
*For if I do not leave you*
*You will break my bloomin' heart*

# DRINKING SONG
## Lyrics by George Reilly

*Chorus: They keep us amused with alcohol
And there's nothing to do here but work, drink and brawl.*

*They sold us a paradise but gave us the Ore
And we work and we drink and we fight all the more.*

*The depression in Glasgow made us all unemployed
Then just when our lives were almost destroyed
We came down to Corby to work for our pay
But there's nothing to do here but drink it away.*

*Chorus: They keep us amused with alcohol
And there's nothing to do here but work, drink and brawl.*

*The camps smell of sweat and you can't call them home
And it's hard to keep your temper in a bar on your own
They work us until eight or nine at night
Is it any wonder we drink and we fight?*

*Chorus: They keep us amused with alcohol
And there's nothing to do here but work, drink and brawl.*

# RESERVOIR SONG
## Lyrics by George Reilly

*With the rumours all killed and The Works almost built*
*There must be no room left for doubt*
*For the Candle must burn and the Tubemills must turn*
*And turn in the middle of a drought.*

*The chairman has said "Without water we're dead*
*Without water our future is grim"*
*So we dammed the Eyebrook*
*And with the water we took*
*Filled the reservoir up to the brim.*

*Chorus: We've come too far now*
*To let the Steelworks run dry*
*It's too late to think of defeat*
*Corby depends on its water supply*
*It's the water makes Corby complete.*

*We came to the town with no water around*
*And a Steelworks to run and supply*
*We couldn't have gone far with no reservoir*
*The Steelworks must never run dry.*

*Chorus: We've come too far now*
*To let the Steelworks run dry*
*It's too late to think of defeat*
*Corby depends on its water supply*
*It's the water makes Corby complete.*

# ACCIDENTS
## Lyrics by Ian Cameron

*What have we done to deserve this life we are living?*
*Why should it be cheaper to die than to live?*
*For the compensation's pennies, and the Workers they are many*
*And who gives a damn for the likes of me and you?*

*You come to your Work and you go about your business*
*You walk over planks as you have done for years*
*But when there's a weak one you are thrown into boiling steam*
*No-one could have saved you even if they had seen.*

*He's done it so many times the excuse it is given*
*But does that make it right to lose one man's life?*
*When the Molten Iron splashes and the Workers they are burned*
*What excuses cover scars and limbs that are gone?*

*As the molten river bursts its banks, the Steelmen they are stranded*
*And the sparks burn their skin and the smoke sears their throats*
*What can you say to widows and children of victims?*
*You can't replace a father with a handful of notes.*

*There's fourteen men working on the side of a Furnace*
*And the gas creeps up on them like some deadly weed*
*When the only thing to save them has to be brought from London*
*Can saving only ten men compensate for their greed?*

*Here the accidents are many, no matter how large or small*
*When one man has gone there's ten more to take his place*
*Now Corby has its mortuary and The Works it helps to fill it*
*How many years must pass until somebody cares?*

*The Unions are trying, The Works is getting safer*
*And mostly we only lose limbs instead of lives*
*But what about the ghost shift who will never leave here*
*Will they wander the site long after we've gone?*

# AS THE WORKS GROWS, SO THE TOWN GROWS

*From cities and the Industries*
*From Scotland they came*
*They all arrived at Kettering*
*Having travelled down by train*
*Then to Corby on another train*
*No-one would go by bus*
*They're unreliable, undependable*
*Not even worth a cuss*

*There is nothing here, nothing to do*
*Nowhere to go or play*
*There are no roads, there are no lights*
*And nowhere to pray*
*No tenements, no corner shops*
*Just pubs to drink your fill*
*And miles of fields and open space*
*With plenty time to kill*

*Chorus: As The Works grows*
*So the town grows*
*One relying on the other*
*And if one dies, they both die*
*Just as if they had been lovers*

*The houses down in Stevie Way*
*Have gardens to be dug*
*It's the first time for many*
*It could become a drug*
*For in Scotland there's no garden*
*No room, just discontent*
*And now there's mouths to feed and things to grow*
*We need an allotment*

*Down in Bessemer and Kelvin Grove*
*The houses they appear*
*Also East Carlton where the staff live*
*The difference it is clear*
*We have the pubs to enjoy ourselves*
*But still nowhere to pray*
*What we need now are some churches*
*This means we're here to stay*

*Chorus*

*The Catholic Church now's established*
*It's going to expand*
*And the Scots have raised six thousand pounds*
*Their church it will be grand*
*But the Baptist and Congregational Church*
*They still have far to go*
*So they'll meet in Messrs Lloyds Cinema*
*But they're biding time, you know*

*With the churches, houses, graveyards too*
*The town it has been born*
*With the Scots in the majority*
*It didn't take them long*
*For if you come from Stevie Way*
*It's just like being home*
*Now you live in Little Scotland*
*There is no need to roam!*

# HAPPY TOWN OF STEEL
## Words and music by Bobby Civil

This song was used as a recruiting song by Stewarts and Lloyds as they toured the West Coast of Scotland looking for Workers. John Wood-Cowling first heard it in the Music Hall in Aberdeen in 1963.

With splendid irony, it was played through the loud-hailers on top of John Carr's support vehicle during the March to London as the Steelworkers entered each new town.

*Travelled through the country*
*I've been to many a town*
*Lived in many cities*
*And one place I have found*
*In sleepy old Northamptonshire*
*No-one knows we're living here*
*They've just heard it's north of London town.*

*Chorus: Oh won't you come to Corby*
*Tell you how we feel*
*Come to Corby*
*A happy town of Steel*

*One man's name was Stewart*
*Another one was Lloyd*
*Came along to Corby*
*To keep the men employed*
*By making Steel from Iron Ore*
*Everyone was very sure*
*They could build a home once more in Corby*

*Chorus*

*Well they built a village*
*Into a town*
*People came from miles around*
*On arrival found a happy town of Steel at Corby*

*Now the population is 50,000 strong*
*Many different Industries*
*All being passed along*
*If you want a place to go*
*I've told you of this town I know*
*Come along and say hello to Corby*

*Chorus: Oh won't you come to Corby*
*Tell you how we live*
*Come to Corby*
*We've got so much to give*
*Oh won't you come to Corby*
*Tell you how we feel*
*Come to Corby*
*A happy town of Steel*

*Oh won't you come to Corby*
*Tell you how we feel*
*Come to Corby*
*A happy town of Steel*

## AUDIENCE FEEDBACK FROM EAST CARLTON PARK
## JULY 2006

"Thank you very much for a very enjoyable evening. The interaction and moving around added to the atmosphere and authenticity. I really felt part of the production. Being still employed by Corus made it even more meaningful. Thank you." - Ann McCarran


"So, so good!!! The best is yet to come then, this is just the beginning. Let's take this out to the wider community - schools would benefit - working environment too." - Anonymous


"Thoroughly enjoyable, Should be compulsory viewing for all those involved in regenerating Corby." - David Green, Manager, Land Securities


"It was fantastic, brought back lots of memories." - Anonymous

"I hope there will be a video to show my friends! Brought back lots of memories, I cried. My mother was unhappy when she first came to Corby. She missed the trees. She would stand on the toilet seat and look out of the window to see a tree. I told her Corby didn't have a heart because people had left their heart behind them. I was five years old when I came to Corby. I have never felt a part of Corby until I saw this play. Now I realise Corby is my life and I really do belong here."
- P.P.J. Scott and Val


"GREAT - really well done - I know how much it must have taken to put on!"
- Anonymous


"Love the photographs, videos and the people. Here for the past, the present and the future." - Anonymous


"Thank you so much - not a Corby girl but have to say this was one of the best pieces of theatre I have ever seen. I felt totally drawn in by it - there is a great future for Corby! X" - Anonymous


"There were a couple of technical things that probably only I would notice. Anyway it wasn't a matter of you doing justice to images but the other way round. Really impressed by *Women of Steel* in many ways. Think it's one of the best things you've done, soon to be beaten by something else I imagine - *Energy in Motion*?

Probably most impressive part was how you managed to pull it all together. It was clear what a huge amount of work went into it. Pretty disgusting that it wasn't funded properly.

Corby Women's Theatre Group - very good. Confused by Lorraine - I eventually realised it was her, but it wasn't her as she was so well in character. Also the woman who played Maggie Thatcher was completely different to her other roles. Proper acting. Scripts all very good.

I know from past experience what a pain in the arse marquees are. Not sure how you managed it but glad you didn't let difficulties stop you. WonderWorld bit was smart.

Thought Shout! were really good - especially Home Bargains line. Had just about the right mix of everything; well researched, some humour, some sadness. Really liked little bits which had loaded meaning specific to certain people but not distracting for others.

One of my tutors used to criticise me for this - that there was 'too much' to understand it all fully. Obviously that's bollocks and something to aspire to. Think you ticked nearly all the Corby Zone aims and objectives.

Top, top quality Arts. Left me with a feeling of pride about Corby. Proper history. Well done again. You know I don't normally give proper compliments but will make an exception this time." - Anonymous

"Fantastic, true life. I am Corby-born and learned so much I did not know from the play. The venue was perfect. There was five in my company, all old Corby and they all enjoyed it." - Anonymous

"I know more wanted to see it so if there is any chance to have it staged in the Willows in Corby it would be wonderful for more to experience what we did." - Jacqui Licquorish

"My partner was there as a First Aider and told me it was fantastic. I was so sorry not to have seen it. I hope it comes out in video. I will definitely buy one." - Anonymous

"Dear Paula
I know it must seem like a long time ago now but I thought I would drop you a line anyway. Despite the inclement weather, I really enjoyed the evening at East Carlton. I thought it was an exceptional event in all sorts of ways. I was particularly impressed with your Women of Steel Theatre Group members who were absolutely brilliant. Well done!" - David Tristram

"Anybody who wants to learn about Corby's history should have gone to see that play. I hope it comes out in video and can be used as a learning tool in the schools. Talk about bringing history to life!" - May Barclay

"Special spirit that makes town unique." - Anonymous

"I congratulate Corby Women's Theatre on its magnificent production of *Women Of Steel*. The Writer and Director (Paula Boulton), players, musicians and all those who helped deserve the highest praise. It was like re-living a real experience by real people.

As a person who has recently moved to Corby, I found the experience very moving and informative. The bits of information which I had picked up over the years of visiting Corby all came together in a very coherent and touching manner.

As a member of the audience, one could feel the feelings of those present – struggle, loneliness, pain, sadness, disappointment, betrayal, survival and much more. Yet out of those hard experiences emerged a very special spirit of generosity and friendship that makes Corby such a unique town.

Indeed, *Women of Steel* has done much to help me identify with the town and its great people.

Perhaps the most striking aspect of the performance related to the closure of the Steelworks and all the consequences that ensued. It did not break the spirit of the people of this town who deserve great admiration.

The future now looks very bright and prosperous. Let's hope the Steel Kids so rightly represented in *Women of Steel* take advantage of the opportunities now offered by this Government and council.

I salute the *Women of Steel* team. This play deserves national exposure."
- Eamonn J. Norton, Stanier Road, Corby

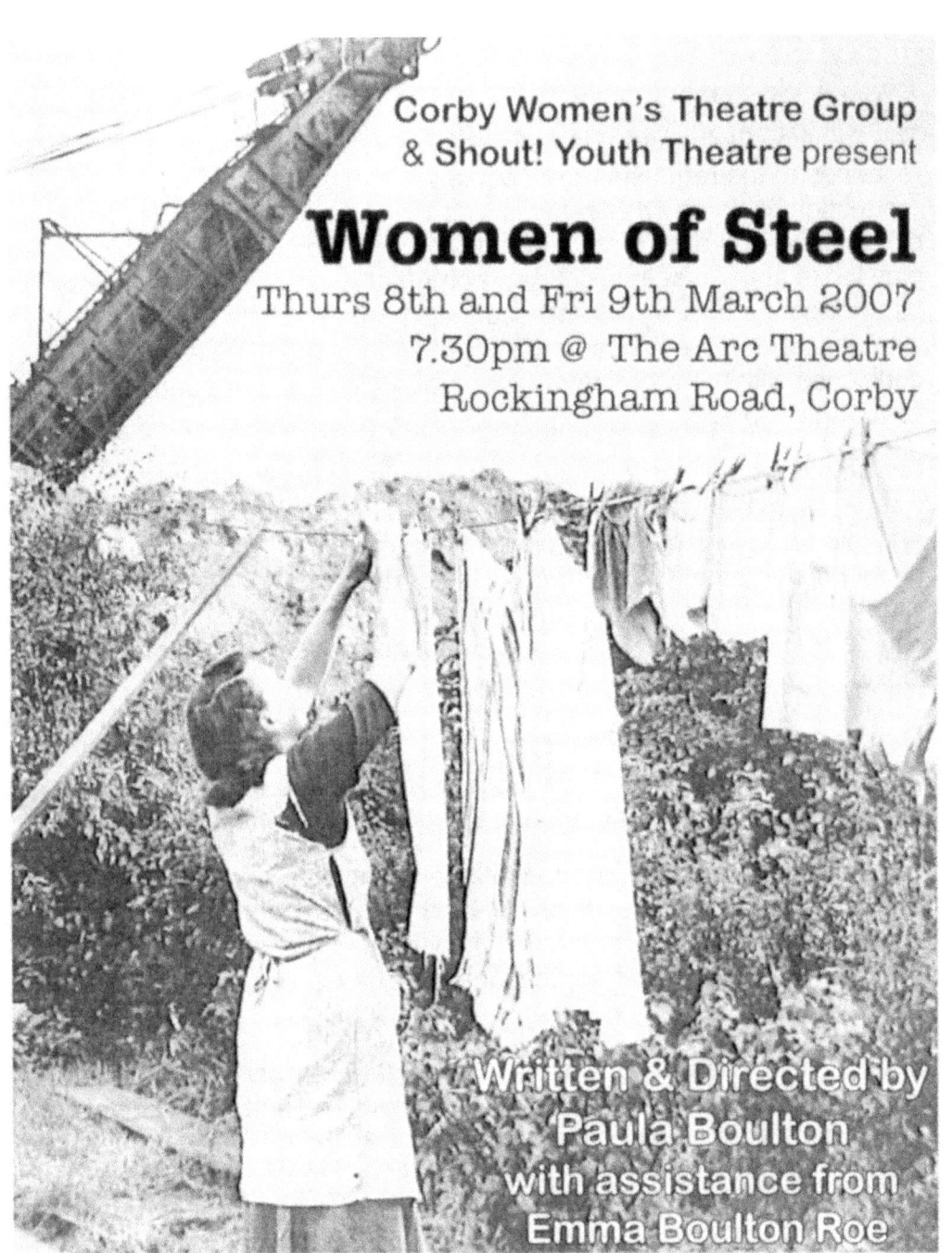

## About the Play

This multimedia theatre adaptation of Women Of Steel was written in response to the requests from people who missed the original outdoor production. Women Of Steel was written to commemorate the closure of the Steel works in Corby in 1980. Through the eyes of women, the play looks at the first influx of new communities in the 30's and takes us through the heyday of Steel production, the battle to Save Steel, the Wonderworld of the 80's, and the depression of the middle years, and concludes with the promise of regeneration, as seen through the eyes of young people.

Playwright and director Paula Boulton says "In writing the play I wanted to look at where we are 25 years since closure, honour the struggle to Save Steel, and acknowledge the fact that hard working people have come to Corby from all over the world for 70 years. Sharing our rich history with the new Corby people will show them they can be proud of the town they have chosen to live in, and join us in looking to a great future."

## Performers and People

Corby Women's Theatre Group formed in September 2004 to create this play, which was first staged at East Carlton Park in July 2006.

Originally the group was funded in an evening class by the Workers Educational Association, which enabled Paula Boulton to share the entire process of 'creating a community drama'. Over 25 women have been part of the group at some stage, and have all contributed their life experiences to the process.

Shout! Youth Theatre, of which all 3 younger performers were members, was formed in 1998 by Paula Boulton and Emma Boulton Roe. Emma wrote the section of the play that looks at how it was to grow up in Corby since steel. Shout! regularly creates unique pieces of theatre as commissioned, such as their play about teenage pregnancy, 'To Do Or Not To Do' which they toured around Northamptonshire libraries.

If you are interested in joining either group contact Paula 01536741922

Our guest performers are former steel workers who walked to London with the Save Steel petition.

# Performers

**Shout! Youth Theatre**
Joris Alexander
Georgia Britton
Robert Cain
Lee Docherty
Tony Giles
Kirsty Graham
Philip Jennings
Terri Langley
Jodie Mallett
Kirsty O'Neil
Amy Pointer
Jennifer Pyper
Jack Boulton Roe
Danielle Skillen
Leanne Villette
Shareace White

**Corby Women's Theatre Group**
Jo Alderson
Paula Boulton
Lorraine Dziarkowska
Irene Hamilton
Betty MacPherson
Margaret Marshall
Kim McGowan
Bridie Norton
Emma Boulton Roe
Jennifer Ross
Lorraine Scatterty
Julie Steventon
Joy Elizabeth Sugery
with guest appearances from:
Crystal Dziarkowska
Steel Men: Peter McGowan
W 'Monty' Monteith

## Organisational Team

| | |
|---|---|
| Stage Manager | Jenny Garlick |
| Assistant Stage Manager | Sue Rainbow |
| Front of House Team | Jack Boulton Roe, Louise Boyle, Micha Davis, Crystal Dziarkowska, Leanne Villette |
| Project Manager | Marian Anderson |

## Creative & Technical Team

| | |
|---|---|
| Costume | Rebecca Boulton Roe |
| Props & Set | Jenny Garlick |
| Programme Design | Corby Community Arts & Marian Anderson |
| Visual Script | Lorraine Dziarkowska, Sami Scott Andy Eathorne & Paula Boulton |
| Technical assistants | Nick Maple & Andrew Maple |
| Sound editing and projection | Sami Scott |
| Video editing | Sami Scott with Andy Eathorne & PVP |
| Videographer | Joy Oliver |
| Photographers | Kenny Martin & Rein Kybarsepp |

## Music

All of the songs from this performance are available on CD.
*Keep the Candle Burning* by Mike Carver, *Happy Town of Steel* by Bobby Civil, *Sweatshop & Broken Dreams* by Banner Theatre, *Wonderworld* by Ian Cameron. All other songs written and composed by The Orebits for **It Starts With The Ore** produced in 1985.

## How it happened

"I finally got the funding for the bulk of this project in December 2005, 18 months after I started! I was ready to give up at that point. The anniversary year had come and gone and my enthusiasm was waning! Until a walk in East Carlton Park and the memory of a wonderful outdoor event collided and I was off again with the idea of writing the play around the heritage centre! Thanks to Jack, Sue and Emma who pushed me to do it, and the women of steel who have stuck with it throughout. I believe between us all we have created something unique which has taken on a life of its own."
*Paula Boulton July 2006*

When Women Of Steel was staged in East Carlton Park in July 2006 it totally sold out, so even though Paula felt she was ready to move on to something new, public and peer pressure mounted for Women Of Steel to happen again.

Corby Women's Theatre Group as a whole felt compelled to offer the play to a wider audience and to present a more enduring version of their creation to the town for future generations.

Paula joined forces with Marian Anderson to seek funding for a wider project 'Stories of Steel' that includes this adaptation of the play for The Arc Theatre and will create of a series of archive materials that will last beyond the actual theatre production.

The launch of the visual and digital archive will take place later this year. A pre-order form is included in this programme so you can express your interest in these items early.

## Research

Thanks to John Wood Cowling, Jim McDonald, Peter McGowan, John Forshaw, Frank Smythe, Mick McGowan, Aidan Coleman, Jane Carr, Peter Floody and Norman Coates.

## Interviewees

Jean Hall, Winnie Scott, Anne-Marie Lawson, Maureen Forshaw, Betty MacPherson, Lorraine Dziarkowska, Joyce Stirling, Carol Lowe, Stanley Boulton, Eda Wood, Shirley White, Rachel Arnold, Sami Scott, the cast and past members of Corby Women's Theatre Group.

# Act 1

Village Life

Roots

Home Sick 1934

The Widow 1960

One Woman Of Steel

Cleaners in the Quantivac 1960

A canteen worker plugmill canteen 1974

As the works grows, so the town grows

Canteen union meeting 1979

R.O.S.A.C. demonstration

The end of steel

**Interval** – refreshments available

# Act 2

Wonderworld Wonderwhen?

Broken Dreams

The Aftermath

Stand Your Ground

Goodbye to Wonderworld

# Act 3

Steel Kids

The Wasted Years (written by Emma Boulton Roe)

Hope for the Future

**The End**

## Stories of Steel

Women Of Steel is part of a wider project funded by Awards For All which includes this theatre adaptation of Women Of Steel and a series of archive materials. If you require any info contact:
Marian Anderson **07946 576 977 marian.anderson@yahoo.co.uk**

## Tribute

We would like to take this opportunity to pay tribute to Richard Carr, NALGO shop steward, and one of the men who walked to London with the Save Steel petition, who was killed tragically earlier this year.

## Corby Women's Refuge

We will be collecting for Corby Women's Refuge on the nights of the play. Corby, the town with the highest rate of domestic violence in the county has been without a refuge since 2000. Several of Corby Women's Theatre group are involved in establishing a new one. This is our chosen charity. The new refuge is now in planning stage and will hopefully be open within a year.

## Thanks

This whole project has been a great team effort. Many people have contributed time and energy to make it a reality – too many people to list. Thanks to Bob Chapman for sharing the vision, ET archivist Liz McBride, East Carlton Park Heritage Centre for providing copies of their archive material, The Lighthouse, Pete Weston, Ruth Tindley, Rotraut Anderson, Corby Trades & Labour Club for rehearsal venue, Julie Steventon and Val Stein for script critique and editing, Jim McClellan & Anne Hanratty at Rockingham Road Primary School/The Arc Theatre, Kingswood Church, Joy Elizabeth Sugery, FORTAC for administrative support, Rocky Road Music for being our official ticket outlet, Corby Borough Council for printing the programme and Corby Women's Theatre Group for matched funding.

**Phil Hope MP**

HOUSE OF COMMONS
LONDON SW1A 0AA

Dear Colleagues,

I am sorry I cannot attend the Women of Steel production this evening - I know from all those who have already seen and performed in it what a local success it has been. I would like to congratulate the women's theatre group for developing and performing this highly acclaimed production once again.

It is a real pleasure that Paula Boulton and the other talented members of Corby Zone are successfully using the arts to convey powerful and inspiring messages. As we enter into an exciting period of regeneration in Corby, it is important that we not only celebrate the physical aspects of renewal but also the social changes in the town - the arts continue to play a vital role in bringing these together.

I am proud of Corby's past. It is vital that we remember our heritage as we look to the future. I was in my twenties at the time of the steel strike. Joining the Corby workers and their families on the marches had a huge impact on my values and beliefs. I will always remember the camaraderie shown by the community in support of the campaign to save jobs and preserve our town.

We have just come through a period where Corby has unfairly taken a 'bashing' in the right wing press. I know that Corby people have spirit and always come back fighting as I witnessed back in the dark days of the 1980s. Economic policy over the last 10 years has brought full employment back to Corby - Women of Steel reminds us not to take for granted the hard fought success we have now achieved.

Yours Sincerely

*Phil Hope.*

Phil Hope MP

**Working for Corby and East Northamptonshire**
**Corby Oundle Thrapston Raunds Irthlingborough**
Constituency Office: Chisholm House, Queens Square, Corby, Northants NN17 1PN
Tel:(01536) 443325 Fax: (01536)269462 E-Mail: hopep@parliament.uk
WebSite: www.philhope.org.uk

# FUNDERS

We would like to thank the following organisations and individuals for their contributions towards the cost of this project.

**LOTTERY FUNDED**

**Awards for All**

**Corus Employees Holiday Savings Scheme**

"Corus employees can elect to have money deducted from their wages each month, to be repaid at holiday times. The savings are held on deposit and the interest is distributed to worthy causes. A workers' committee meets twice yearly to consider applications received.

The scheme has been running since 1980 and in that time has donated nearly £660,000 to worthy local causes. Help has been given in many different areas: Arts, Animal Welfare, Disabled, Medical, Military, Playgroups, Religious, Schools, Scouts & Guides, Senior Citizens, Sports, Village Halls, Welfare and Youth groups.

Annual donations, as a result of the reduced size of the workforce, are not as high as they once were and are currently about £3,000 per year."

**GMB - Britain's General Union** (General Municipal Boilermakers)
GMB Union Corby Community Branch and Midland & East Coast Region. Anyone wishing to join the local branch should contact the recruiting phone number 01159 601113 or the union website www.gmbmidandec.org.uk
Branch Secretary:
Gordon Glassford, GMB Corby Community Branch,
24 Cresswell Walk, Corby, Northants NN17 2LL Tel: 01536 262733

**Kingswood Community Arts Plan**

**Unison Kettering**

**Unite the Union**
(In 2007, Amicus merged with the Transport and General Workers' Union to form Unite the Union).

**Louise Bagshawe, Cllr Julie Brookfield, Phil Hope MP**

# ACKNOWLEDGEMENTS

I would like to thank John Wood-Cowling, ISTC Executive member at The Steelworks from 1975 to 1981, and himself author of the book *Corby, Town of Steel*, for readily sharing so much information with me throughout the writing process.

Also contributors to the book who shared their knowledge, stories or experiences: Bill Martin & John Martin, Andy McCabe, Mags McGuire, Dennis Taylor, Robert Sneddon, Simon Pickvance, Spike the Poet, Ray Beeby, Daniel Boulton, Rose Labuschagne Pereira, Gordon Glassford, CBC housing regeneration team, Sharon Pyper, Jean Butcher, Ann-Marie Lawson, Sean Kettle, Charles Connor, Tommie Beattie, Alan Irwin, Gary Docherty, Tim Cunningham, Alec McKinty, Monty Monteith, Sue Nathan, Jimmy Noble, John Stanley, Ian Merrillees, Evelyn Reilly, Cathy Curran, Ruth Tindley, Joyce Stirling, Rachel Arnold, Tracy Timmins, Michael Kimmins, Rein Kubarsepp, Ellen Allen, Jenny Garlick, Oundle Cinema, Phil Hope, Chris Mallender, Martyn Barr.

**P.E.A.R.L.S**

Treasurers: Irene Hamilton from P.E.A.R.L.S (People Enthusiastic About Real Living), Thea Lumbers from FORTAC (Federation of Residents and Tenants Association Corby) and James Steventon for financial administration.

My co-writers Emma and Jack Boulton Roe for their feedback and opinions, Julie Steventon and Carol Martin for proofreading.

Doug Becker, Jimmy Boulton, Rebecca Boulton, Josie Cassidy, Clare Chacksfield, Digby Chacksfield, Victoria Elizabeth Davies, Paul Henderson, Sean Kettle, Bill Martin, Maggie Saxon, Lorraine Scatterty, Will Smith, James Steventon and Joyce Stirling and CWTHG for critique.

Bonnie Blay and all at Impress Print in Corby for their kind help and assistance throughout the production stages.

Val Stein for her unerring eye for detail, skilful editing and belief in the book.

And last but not least, Kenneth Martin, my publisher and guide, for his experience, dedication and determination to see the project through to completion.

## PHOTO CREDITS

I would like to thank the following people who kindly lent us photographs from their personal collections for inclusion in the *Women of Steel* project:

Bob Mears, Dennis Taylor, Ray Beeby, Monty Monteith, East Carlton Heritage Centre, Madelyn McAlpine, Corby Borough Council, Stewarts and Lloyds, British Steel Corporation.

Corby *Evening Telegraph* Archivists, Liz McBride and Caroline Morgan, and the Editor, Jeremy Clifford, for permission to reproduce the ET articles that appear in the book.

Thanks to Lyn Plumpton, Jan Timmins, Lorraine Dziarkowska, Sami Scott and Andy Eathorne for input on image work. Kenneth Martin for digital re-touching.

Dr Peter Hill for permission to include twelve photographs from his own books (see Bibliography / Further Reading for details of these).

I would like to thank the following Photographers for their work on the project: Lorraine Dziarkowska, Kate Dyer & Corby Community Arts, Sulev Koppel, Rein Kubarsepp, Kenneth Martin and Lyn Plumpton.

Thanks to the *Women of Steel* cast for photographs from their personal family albums.

## INDIVIDUAL PHOTO CREDITS

| | |
|---|---|
| Cover | "Washing Women" from Ron Sismey's *Corby: A Pictorial History* |
| p.7 | "Wild Deer Roaming (Welland Valley)" Kenneth Martin, 2008 |
| p.18 | "Three Generations of Welsh Miners" W. Eugene-Smith, 1950 |
| p.51 | "Tools of the Trade (Mop and Bucket)" Kenneth Martin, 2007 |
| p.119 | "Dockers" courtesy of the TUC website archive |
| p.126 | "Commonwealth Immigrants, 1948" Science & Society Picture Library |
| p.129 | (bottom) "Sewing Machinists" Kevin Hayes |
| p.142 | "Travel photos: Australia, New Zealand, Thailand" 6 photos, Alison Hannah |
| p.142 | (top right) "Ireland" Rachel Arnold |
| p.143 | "Travel Photomontage" 9 photographs from Nepal, Kenneth Martin, 2006 |
| p.150 | (bottom) "Lake Phewa Tal, Pokhara, Nepal" Kenneth Martin, 2006 |
| p.159 | "The Future" (Act Two, Scene 7) Slideshow designed by James Steventon |
| p.210 | "Orgreave Coke Works Picket Miners' Strike" John Harris, 18th June 1984 |
| p.225 | "Million Women Rise" courtesy of www.socialistunity.com |
| p.226 | "Scenic Scotland" Kenneth Martin, 2007 |

Every effort has been made to contact copyright holders, and apologies are offered if any such ownership has not been acknowledged.

# BIBLIOGRAPHY / FURTHER READING

Some of the source books referred to during the making of *Women of Steel* are listed below.

Alan Irwin
*The Wasted Years* (self-published, 1991)

John Wood-Cowling
*Corby, Town of Steel: a personal view of the 1980 Closure of Steelmaking in Corby*
Privately published on CD-ROM in the form of a book in HTML format.
Available for £6.00 to cover duplication and postage costs.
Info: j.woodcowling@tiscali.co.uk or ray.rodden@orange.net

Allen Maunders
*A process of struggle. The campaign for Corby Steelmaking in 1979.*
(Gower, 1987)

Ian Addis and Robert Mercer (eds)
*Corby Remembers: A century of memories, 100 years of change*
(Diametric, 2000)

Ron Sismey
*Corby: A Pictorial History* (Phillimore, 1993)

Peter Hill
*Corby: Pocket Images,* (Nonsuch, 2007) previously published as:
*Corby: The Second Selection* (Tempus, 1998)
*Corby: The Archive Photographs Series* (Tempus, 1995)
*Corby: Living Memories* (The Frith Collection, 2002)

British Steel Corporation
*Corby Works, Ironmaking: Maintenance Induction Manual* (BSC, 1978)

www.ingramcontent.com/pod-product-compliance
Lightning Source LLC
Chambersburg PA
CBHW081407080526
44589CB00016B/2486